CW00665902

Aada[...]
Muaasharat
Etiquettes of Social Life

Maulvi Ashraf Ali Thanvi (Ra.)

www.idaraimpex.com

© Idara Impex

No Part of this book may be reproduced or utilised in any form
or by any means, electronic or mechanical including photo
copying, recording or by any information storage and retrieval
system without permission in writing from the Publisher.

Aadaabul Muaasharat
Etiquettes of social life

Maulana Ashraf Ali Thanvi (Ra.)

ISBN 81-7101-145-4

Edition 2015

TP-420-15

Published by Mohammad Yunus for
IDARA IMPEX
D-80, Abul Fazal Enclave-I, Jamia Nagar
New Delhi-110 025 (India)
Tel.: 2695 6832 Fax: +91-11-6617 3545
Email: **sales@idaraimpex.com**
Visit us at: **www.idarastore.com**
Designed & Printed in India

Retail Shop: **IDARA IMPEX**
Shop 6, Nizamia Complex, Gali Gadrian, Hazrat Nizamuddin
New Delhi-110013 (India) Tel.: 085888 44786

CONTENTS

PAGE NO.

INTRODUCTION

MUAASHARAT or social conduct - the way the Muslim has to behave in society - is the subject matter of the kitaab, AADAABUL MUAASHARAT *(ETIQUETTES OF SOCIAL LIFE)* written by Hakimul Ummat Hadhrat Maulana Ashraf Ali Thaanvi (rahmatullah alayh). The book is presented in simple form and has been prepared for every Muslim, of whatever walk of life.

Muaasharat is a sorely lacking dimension in the Muslim community of the time, wherever it prevails. Under the impact of the onslaught of westernism aggravated by gross ignorance of Islam, Muslims remain largely ignorant of Islamic social conduct. This book reminds Muslims in simple language of the Islamic requirements in the domain of social life. Without correct Muaasharat it is not possible to develop a healthy Islamic community. Muaasharat has in fact been divinely ordained for engendering harmony, love, peace and cohesion among the members of the community. Abandonment of Islamic Muaasharat has ushered in all the baneful traits and attitudes of a materialized western culture devoid of all lofty and transcendental values.

It is imperative for every Muslim to study and implement the advices and direction offered by Hakimul Ummat.

All advices contained herein are raised on the Qur'aan, the Sunnah and sound Shar'i principles. There is no theory here. Everything in the book is for practical expression. Without practical adoption of Islamic Muaasharat, the culture of the Qur'aan and Sunnah is not possible.

MUJLISUL ULAMA OF SOUTH AFRICA
P.O. BOX 3393
PORT ELIZABETH
6056
SOUTH AFRICA

Muharram 1411
August 1990

1

بسم الله الرحمن الرحيم
نحمده ونصلي على رسوله الكريم

THE FIVE BRANCHES

Of the five constitutional branches of Islam Muslims in general nowadays regard only two branches as being integral parts of the Deen. These are Aqaa-id (beliefs) and Ibaadaat (worship). The Ulama-e-Zaahir (those Ulama concerned only with the external dimension of Islam - with only the letter of the law) consider the third branch, viz. Muamalaat (mutual dealings and transactions) also an integral part of Deen. The Mashaaikh (of Tasawwuf) consider the fourth branch, viz. Akhlaaq (Moral character) also part of the Deen. However, the fifth branch, viz. Aadaabul Muasharat (Social Etiquette) has been excluded from the Deen by all three groups, excepting a few among them. In fact, it is believed that this branch is totally unrelated to the Deen. This is the view of the majority. It is precisely for this reason that the other branches of the Deen are more or less all dealt with and discussed in lectures and discourses. On the contrary, no mention whatever is made of this fifth branch (Muasharat). Hence, this branch has been assigned to the limbo of oblivion both theoretically and practically.

The main cause for the dissipation of mutual love and affection is corrupt behavioural attitudes. As a result of such corruption of behaviour and manners mutual resentment and dislike for one another have set in among people. This state of affairs impedes and eliminates tranquility of heart which is of pivotal importance for mutual love in the members of society.

The Qur'aan, Ahadith and the statements of the Wise men refute the claim that this branch (Social Etiquette) has no relationship with the Deen. Some of these statements shall be cited here in substantiation.

*Allah Ta'ala says:
"O People of Imaan! When it is said to you to give space in a gathering, then make space. When it is said to you: Stand up!, then stand up."
(Qur'aan)
"O People of Imaan! Do not enter homes besides your own homes as long as you have not sought permission and greeted the inmates of the houses. That is best for you so that you ponder.
Then, if you do not find any one therein (in the homes), do not enter therein unless permission is granted to you. And, if it is said to you: 'Return!', then turn back. That is purest for you. Allah knows well what you are doing."

2

These verses exhort consideration for others, for those who happen to be present in a gathering and for the inmates of the house.

* Rasulullah (sallallahu alayhi wasallam) ordered that while eating in company one should not take two dates at a time without having obtained the consent of one's friends. Such an insignificant act has been prohibited solely on account of disrespect and because of dislike which this act will engender in others.

* Rasulullah (sallallahu alayhi wasallam) said that the one who eats raw garlic and onions should remain aloof from us. Since the odour will be annoying to others, Rasulullah (sallallahu alayhi wasallam) forbade this insignificant act.

* Rasulullah (sallallahu alayhi wasallam) said that it is not lawful for a guest to stay for such a length of time which imposes a difficulty on the host. In this prohibition, an act which causes inconvenience to others has been proscribed.

* Rasulullah (sallallahu alayhi wasallam) said that when eating in company one should continue eating until the others have completed even though one has eaten to satiation.
By discontinuing to eat, those who are still eating are put to shame. It is thus clear that one should not act in any way which embarrasses others. Some people, on account of natural shame, refrain from taking something in a gathering although they wish for it. Others again feel it difficult to refuse a request in a gathering although they have no desire of giving. Such persons should not be given things in a gathering nor should anything be asked of them in a gathering.

* In the Hadith it is narrated that once Hadhrat Jaabir (radhiallahu anhu) came to the house of Rasulullah (sallallahu alayhi wasallam). On knocking at the door, Rasulullah (Sallallahu alayhi wasallam) enquired: "Who is it?"
Jaabir (radhiallahu anhu) replied: "It is me." Rasulullah (sallallahu alayhi wasallam) in annoyance, said:
"It is me. It is me." From this we learn that statements should not be made ambiguously. One should speak with clarity to enable the listener to fully understand. Ambiguous statements which cause confusion perturb people.

* Hadhrat Anas (radhiallahu anhu) stated that there was no person dearer to the Sahaabah than Rasulullah (sallallahu alayhi wasallam). Inspite of this, he says the Sahaabah would not stand in respect for Rasulullah (sallallahu alayhi wasallam) because of his aversion for this mode of respect. This establishes that any etiquette, way of respect or any form of service which is

3

displeasing to a person should not be rendered to him. One should give priority to the wishes and feelings of others, not to one's own desires. Some people by their insistence to render certain acts of service to the Auliya are in actual fact inconveniencing them.

* Rasulullah (sallallahu alayhi wasallam) said that it is not permissible for a person to intrude in the company of two people without obtaining their consent. Such intrusion constricts the hearts. Thus, it is necessary to abstain from acts and attitudes which inhibit or cause inconvenience to others.

* According to the Hadith, Rasulullah (sallallahu alayhi wasallam) would cover his mouth with his hand or a handkerchief when sneezing. In this way he stifled the sound to avoid causing annoyance to others. This establishes that one should not annoy or scare or inconvenience one's companions by means of loudness and shouting.

* Hadhrat Jaabir (radhiallahu anhu) narrates that the Sahaabah would sit down in any place where they reached in the gathering of Rasulullah (sallallahu alayhi wasallam). They would not pass through others in order to obtain seating place ahead. This attitude of the Sahaabah establishes the aadaab (etiquettes) of a majlis (gathering). The slightest inconvenience to others was avoided.

* Hadhrat Ibn Abbaas, Hadhrat Saeed Bin Musayyib and Hadhrat Anas (radhiallahu anhum) narrate in ahadith of different categories that when visiting the sick one should not remain for a long time. The visit should be short. This narration indicates the degree to which one should go in refraining from inconveniencing others. Sometimes a sick person due to his condition suffers inconvenience by the lengthy presence of others. However, the presence of such persons who are a source of comfort and solace to the sick are excluded from this prohibition.

* Hadhrat Ibn Abbaas (radhiallahu anhu), explaining the reason for the need to take ghusl (bath) on Fridays, says that in the initial period of Islam most people were poor labourers. Soiled garments and perspiration caused bad odours. Hence ghusl was decreed waajib (obligatory) in the beginning. Later, the incumbency (wujoob) was abrogated and ghusl for Jumma' was retained as a Sunnat act. It thus transpires that it is incumbent to refrain from causing the slightest inconvenience and annoyance to anyone.

* In Sunan Nisaai there appears a narration in which Hadhrat Aishah (radhiallahu anha) speaks of Rasulullah's (sallallahu alayhi wasallam) exit from the house on the Night of Baraa'at. He opened the door silently so as

4

not to disturb the sleeping ones. Similarly he closed the door silently. He did not commit any act which produced the slightest noise. He totally abstained from any disturbance to ensure that no one's sleep is disturbed nor anyone be suddenly awakened.

* In a lengthy hadith in Sahih Muslim, Hadhrat Miqdaad (radhiallahu anhu) says that once a group of them were the guests of Rasulullah (sallallahu alayhi wasallam). After Isha the guests would go to bed. Rasulullah (sallallahu alayhi wasallam), on arriving much later, would make salaam (greet) in such a whisper that if anyone was awake he could hear and if anyone was asleep he would not be disturbed thereby. This Hadith as well indicates the lengths to which Rasulullah (sallallahu alayhi wasallam) would go in order to refrain from causing the slightest inconvenience to others.

Numerous similar narrations bear ample testimony to this fact.

* In the narrations of Fiqh *(Jurisprudence)* it is categorically stated that one should not greet a person who is engaged in eating, teaching, etc. From this it emerges that according to the Shariah it is detestable to divert the mind or attention of a person who is engaged in some necessary activity.

* The Fuqaha have ruled that it is permissible to prevent from the Musjid a person who suffers from the disease of bad odour emitting from the mouth. It is quite clear from these examples that it is essential to prevent anything which is a cause of inconvenience or annoyance to others.

A comprehensive perusal of these proofs (of the Qur'aan and Hadith) very clearly shows that the Shariat has established a very lofty system of life in which no facet of man's behaviour, attitudes and actions will constitute the slightest difficulty, harm, displeasure, detestation and ill-feeling to another fellow being. His behaviour should not be a cause of worry, confusion or fear to anyone. In this regard Rasulullah (sallallahu alayhi wasallam) did not confine this lofty attitude and behaviour to only his own statements and acts, but whenever any among his close companions displayed the slightest neglect in this matter, he would compel them to observe correct behaviour. Furthermore, Rasulullah (sallallahu alayhi wasallam) practically demonstrated this lofty degree of behaviour by the imposition of tasks and duties on the Sahaabah. A Sahaabi once presented a gift to Rasulullah (sallallahu alayhi wasallam). However, he entered the presence of Rasulullah (sallallahu alayhi wasallam) without permission and without greeting.

Rasulullah (sallallahu alayhi wasallam) ordered:
"Go out; say Assalamu Alaikum, may I enter?"

5

In actual fact the secret underlying beautiful conduct with people is to save them from inconvenience and annoyance. Rasulullah (sallallahu alayhi wasallam) summed up this lofty concept of behaviour and conduct most beautifully and comprehensively in the following Hadith:

"The true Muslim is he from whose tongue and hand Muslims are safe."

Any act which causes inconvenience, annoyance or difficulty is an act of misbehaviour even though it may ostensibly be financial aid, physical labour or honour and respect according to general prevalent custom because comfort is the soul of good character, and this has priority over service which in actual fact is the outer shell. The shell minus the kernel is obviously useless.

Although the Department of Muasharat (Social Etiquette) is posterior to the Departments of Aqaaid (Beliefs) and Ibaadaat-e-Fareedhah (Compulsory acts of worship), nevertheless, since a rupture in Aqaaid and Ibaadaat brings about personal detriment while a rupture in Muasharat results in harm to others, the latter will enjoy priority over the former two from this angle. Harming others is graver than harming oneself. In Surah Furqaan Allah Ta'ala says:

"They walk on earth in humility and when the ignorant ones address them, they say: Salaam."

This aayat indicates Beautiful Conduct (Husn Muasharat) and it appears before mention is made of Salaat, Fear, Tauheed and moderation in spending. Afterall, there must be some reason for the Qur'aan according it priority over the Department of Aqaaid and Ibaadaat-e-Fareedhah. This priority over Fardh (compulsory) acts of worship is in regard to certain matters. However, in sofar as Nafl acts of Ibaadat are concerned, Muasharat has greater emphasis in all respects. Thus, the condition of two women was explained to Rasulullah (sallallahu alayhi wasallam). One woman while engaging in abundant Salaat, Saum (Fasting) and Thikr was in the habit of causing difficulty and inconvenience to her neighbours. The other woman, although not engaging in an abundance of Salaat and Saum, refrained from harming her neighbours. Rasulullah (sallallahu alayhi wasallam) described the first woman as an inmate of Jahannam and the second woman as an inmate of Jannat.

Although Muasharat does not take precedence over Muamalaat (transactions and contracts) in this respect since a rupture in Muamalaat also results in harm to others, it (Muasharat) nevertheless enjoys priority over Muamalaat from another angle. Only the elite (the Ulama) consider the Department of Muamalaat to be an integral part of Deen. On the otherhand, only the special among the elite regard Muasharat to be included in the

6

Deen. Many among the elite do not regard Muasharat as being part of the Deen. Although some among them do consider Muasharat to be part of the Deen, they do not regard it as important as the Department of Muamalaat. It is for this very reason that very little practical acceptance is accorded to Muasharat. The reformation of the baatin *(the nafs)* has the same order (hukm) as compulsory acts of Ibaadat. The angle of priority which was explained earlier applies in this case as well, i.e. priority of Muasharat over Muamalaat.

Inspite of the great importance of Muasharat, numerous people among the general public and some among the Ulama as well offer extremely little attention to it for practical purposes. Even those who give practical expression to Muasharat, totally abstain from instructing others in this regard. This state of affairs engendered in me the desire sometime ago to write something on Aadaab-e-Muasharat with which I am confronted at most times. For quite a long time now I have been verbally admonishing and directing those associated with me. In most lectures too I emphasise on these matters. There has been a great delay in preparing this treatise. In the Knowledge of Allah Ta'ala the time for this treatise has been ordained for the present.

I have compiled this treatise without according much regard to systematic order. I wrote as things came to mind. If this treatise is taught to children and even to elders, then, Insha'Allah, the pleasure of Jannat will be experienced right here on earth.

THE FIVE BRANCHES OF THE SHARIAT

The Shariat consists of five branches or parts:
Aqaa-id, A'maal, Muamalaat, Akhlaaq, Husn-e-Muasharat.

AQAA-ID *(Beliefs)*, e.g. beliefs in the Oneness of Allah Ta'ala and the Risaalat *(Prophethood)* of Rasulullah (sallallahu alayhi wasallam).

A'MAAL *(Righteous deeds)* e.g. Salaat, Saum.

MUAMALAAT *(Transactions, Contracts)* e.g. trade and commerce.

AKHLAAQ *(Moral character)* e.g. humility, generosity, etc.

HUSN-E-MUASHARAT *(Beautiful social conduct)*, i.e. good relationship with people, e.g. abstention from acts which cause others inconvenience, such as disturbing a person in his sleep.

The above mentioned five departments are collectively known as the Shariat. It is essential for Muslims to adopt all five departments of the Shariat. But, in the present age people have abbreviated the Shariat. Some have taken only Aqaa-id, believing that only the proclamation of *La ilaaha il lallaahu* suffices for immediate entry into Jannat. Such persons, while they believe Salaat, Saum, etc., are Fardh, they do not obtain the good fortune of practically executing these acts of worship. Others again, along with Aqaa-id observe Salaat, Saum, etc., as well. However, they have discarded Muamalaat. In their transactional dealings they are not concerned with the Deen, whether their acts are lawful or not. They are indifferent to the question of halaal and haraam regarding their earnings and dealings. Then there are those who maintain their Muamalaat on a healthy footing, but are unconcerned with the reformation of their moral character. Those who are concerned about Akhlaaq are exceptionally few. In fact there are even such persons who spend considerable time to reform others while others are inconvenienced and annoyed by their behaviour and attitude. They remain unaware of the difficulty they are causing others by their actions and behaviour. They are completely uncaring about their own detestable condition. There are numerous such persons who will not venture to offer Salaam to a poor Muslim along the road. On the contrary they wait in expectation of the Salaam to be initiated by the poor.

Some people, along with Aqaaid, A'maal and Muamalaat are concerned about the reformation of Akhlaaq, hence they adopt ways and measures for the treatment of their morals. But, they have discarded Husn-e-Muasharat. In fact, they have excised it from the Deen. They assert that there is no relationship between the Shariah and social conduct with people.

8

They therefore behave as they please, thinking that the Shariah has no say in such matters. Many people are pious with good qualities such as humility, but in Muasharat they are lacking. They are not concerned whether they annoy and inconvenience others by their behaviour. In most insignificant things they bring about difficulty and inconvenience to others. Their attention is totally diverted from little things which cause difficulty to others while in the Hadith there are numerous incidents narrated which show that Rasulullah (sallallahu alayhi wasallam) cared for the little things just as much as he cared for important matters.

MUASHARAT AN INTEGRAL PART OF THE DEEN

It should now be realized that Muasharat is an inseparable part of the Deen. A perfect Muslim will, therefore, be one who adopts all the branches of the Deen. In all aspects he has to behave like a Muslim. There has to be no resemblance with the kuffaar.

People have generally understood Muamalaat and Muasharat to be beyond the scope of the Deen. It is indeed surprising that a person regards his dealings and his social conduct beyond the confines of Divine Law, but at the same time he acknowledges that his dealings and social conduct are governed by the laws of worldly governments. No one ever ventured to tell the state authorities that the government has no right in our private business enterprises, etc. People readily submit to governmental laws and restrictions applicable to their trade and commerce, etc.

BEAUTIFUL SOCIAL CONDUCT IS MORE IMPORTANT THAN BEAUTIFUL DEALINGS OF COMMERCE

The need for proper observance of Muasharat is of greater importance than Muamalaat. Rectitude in Muamalaat largely ensures the protection of material wealth while Husn-e-Muasharat *(Beautiful conduct with others)* ensures the protection of the hearts of the Muslims. It is quite obvious that the rank of the heart is greater than that of material wealth. In the rectification of Muasharat is also the protection of the honour and reputation of others. After the protection of Imaan, safeguarding honour and reputation is of the greatest importance. Man is prepared to sacrifice everything in the endeavour to safeguard his honour. On the occasion of Hajjatul Wida, Rasulullah (sallallahu alayhi wasallam) declared the sanctity of the blood, honour and wealth of the Muslimeen. Until the Day of Qiyaamah the honour and reputation of the Believers have been declared sacred. This sanctity cannot, therefore, be violated.

9

THE MUASHARAT OF ISLAM IS UNIQUE

Islamic Muasharat has no parallel. There is absolutely no need for Muslims to emulate the conduct of others. Muasharat should not be confused with pompous styles and the possession of material goods of pride and show. Takabbur (pride) and pomp destroy the roots of Muasharat. The proud man desires to be the superior of others. He will, therefore, not deal with others sympathetically and justly. The Islamic teaching of Muasharat, in contrast, inculcates humility in man. Without humility sympathy and unity are not possible. These are, in actual fact, the foundations of Muasharat. True Muasharat is in fact only Islam.

Consider for example, the Islamic conduct pertaining to eating and drinking. Rasulullah (sallallahu alayhi wasallam) demonstrated this conduct both verbally and practically. Thus, he said:

"I eat as a slave eats."

It was the noble character of Rasulullah (sallallahu alayhi wasallam) to eat sitting in a humble position with his body bent. He would eat quickly with relish. In contrast, we eat in great pomp and style. There is not a sign of humility on us when we eat. This type of proud conduct is the consequence of the reality (of life) being hidden from us. When the reality becomes revealed to a person and he realizes that whatever we are eating is from the Court of the King of kings (Ahkamul Haakimeen) and He is observing our every act, then automatically the humble manner of Rasulullah (sallallahu alayhi wasallam) will be adopted. When the greatness of a being is rooted in the heart, then all stages will be traversed with ease. The fact is that we lack the ability to realize that Allah Ta'ala is watching us. He observes our every act. Now when Islam possesses its code of Muasharat in a state of perfection, then what need is there for Muslims to look askance to aliens? Honour, self-respect and our claim of the superiority of our Deen demand that even if our Muasharat was imperfect (on assumption), then too, we should not direct our gaze at alien cultures. Our old and tattered blanket is better than the borrowed shawl of another.

ISLAMIC AND NON-ISLAMIC SOCIAL CONDUCT: A COMPARISON

Even in dressing, our brethren have adopted the conduct and styles of aliens whereas there is no culture which can compare with Islam in matters of dress. Many rules and restrictions govern the dressing styles and garments of non-Muslims. They are supposed to be liberal and they always proclaim the slogan of freedom. But, in actual fact, they are fettered to numerous restrictions in both dress and eating habits and styles. While the

Islamic style of dressing and eating is one of simplicity, the methods and styles of the non-Muslims have many restrictive etiquettes. Indeed their styles are veritable prisons for those imprisoned in elaborate customary rules pertaining to dressing and eating styles.

There are wonderful barkaat *(blessings)* in simplicity. A simple person is saved from many difficulties and hardships. Pomp and pretence bring in their wake numerous difficulties. In contrast, there is sweetness and comfort in simplicity. While everyone desires simplicity and a simple life-style, pride and the thought of disgrace prevent them from adopting a simple conduct of life.

Reformation of Muasharat is imperative since it is an essential branch of the Deen. Just as Salaat and Saum are compulsory, so too is Muasharat incumbent. Nowadays Muasharat is not even considered to be a part of the Deen whereas in the Hadith many chapters have been compiled in this sphere of life. But, no one was prepared to pay any heed to this vital department of the Shariat. After ages has Allah Ta'ala now opened the avenue of reformation.

The Aadaab *(etiquettes)* of Muasharat are continuously disappearing by the day although these are natural things. But, rectitude has in fact vanished from the hearts of people. A greater evil is the laxity of attitude. The capacity to ponder and reflect is absent. If Muslims contemplate, their gaze will reach all sides.

THE REMEDY FOR FRUSTRATION

The Shariat aims to eliminate frustration. In every condition the Shariat endeavours that man is at peace. Whether it be in sorrow or in happiness, it is the Shariat's aim that one should be in the state of peace, not of frustration. The Shariat teaches the way of lightening grief and sorrow. Its teachings regarding peace augment the factors of peace so that these are not destroyed. If the correct principles are adopted, no one will become frustrated. There is no frustration in the Deen whether it be in the realm of *Ahkaam-e-Zaahirah* (the external laws) or *Ahkaam-e-Baatinah* (the internal laws) pertaining to the soul.

THE AADAAB OF SALAAM

(1) In a gathering where a talk or discussion is taking place, the person entering should not draw attention to himself by making salaam. He should not become an interference in the talk. He should lower his gaze and silently sit down. When later the opportunity arises, he may make Salaam.

(2) Adopt the practice of mutual Salaam. Whenever meeting a Muslim, say: ASSALAMU ALAIKUM. In reply say: WA ALAIKUMUS SALAAM.
All other ways are baseless.

(3) When a person conveys the Salaams of another to you, reply: ALAYHIM WA ALAIKUMS SALAAM. This is best. If someone replies: WA ALAIKUMUS SALAAM, it will also suffice.

(4) One person of the group making Salaam will be representative of the whole group. His Salaam will be adequate on behalf of the group. Similarly, if from the gathering one person replied, it will suffice on behalf of the whole gathering.

(5) The one who initiates the Salaam obtains greater thawaab.

(6) When replying to the Salaam of a person, the Salaam should be made verbally, not by a sign of the hand or a nod of the head.

(7) Better repayment for a favour will be when the repayment is somewhat more than the act of favour rendered. Thus, the reply should be more than the Salaam (greeting). If ASSALAMU ALAIKUM was said, the better reply will be WA ALAIKUMUS SALAAM WARAHMATULLAAH. If WA BARAKAA TUHU is also added it will be an added merit.

(8) It is waajib (obligatory) to reply to the Salaam which is written in a letter. This reply may be in writing or verbally.

(9) The Fuqaha have said that in reply to the Salaam which is written in a letter, one may say ALAIKUMUS SALAAM or even ASSALAMU ALAIKUM.

(10) In a letter in which a dua is written, the Salaam should be written first since this is the Sunnat method.

(11) Instead of writing or saying the Salaam, to say any other term or to adopt the greeting of any other community is bid'ah. Such an alien greeting is in fact alteration of the Shariah.

(12) A person who is engrossed in a conversation or in some work should not be greeted. The new-comer should not intrude with his hand-shaking. Such an act is uncultured and causes distress to others.

(13) It is Makrooh to greet a person involved in Deeni or natural activity. Thus, to make Salaam to a person eating is Makrooh while it is not Makrooh to engage in conversation while eating.

(14) It is not permissible to bow and make Salaam.

(15) Before entering a house or any place of privacy it is necessary to seek permission. Do not enter without permission.

(16) Stand outside and proclaim the Salaam, then ask permission in any language. Use such terms which convey the full meaning. However, as far as the Salaam itself is concerned only the terms of the Shariah should be used.

(17) When answering the call of nature neither reply to anyone's Salaam nor offer Salaam.

(18) On promising to convey a person's Salaam, it becomes waajib to do so, otherwise not.

(19) When making Salaam to elders adopt a low voice. Do not express yourself in such terms which convey arrogance or disrespect.

THE AADAAB OF MUSAAFAHAH

(1) Do not shake hands (musaafahah) with a person when his hands are involved in such an act or activity which necessitates his emptying his hands. On such occasions Salaam is adequate. Similarly, when someone (e.g. the leader in a gathering or the Ustaadh or the Shaikh) is engaged in something (e.g. giving a talk), then do not remain standing in expectation of obtaining consent for sitting. Merely be seated.

(2) If someone is hurrying along the road, do not stop him for hand-shaking. Such a person should not be stopped and engaged in conversation. You may be holding him up from something important.

(3) When arriving in a gathering do not make musaafahah with everyone present. Make musaafahah with only the person whom you intend to see.

(4) Some people are under the impression that mere handshaking is sufficient for restoring the peace between two antagonists or persons who have quarrelled. While the malice remains in the hearts musaafahah is of no benefit. Firstly clear the air by solving the dispute. Thereafter make musaafahah.

(5) Musaafahah should be made on arrival and on departure.

(6) When making musaafahah, the hands should not contain anything. Some people holding money in their hands make musaafahah. In this way

13

they present a gift. This is improper. Musaafahah is a Sunnat act which is an Ibaadat. It should not be corrupted with a worldly deed.

(7) Do not wait in expectation of musaafahah. Do not wish that people come forward to shake your hands.

(8) The Sunnat method of musaafahah is only to shake hands. In some places there is the custom of kissing the hands after making musaafahah. This practice should be discontinued.

On the occasion of Hijrat (Migration from Makkah to Madinah) Hadhrat Abu Bakr Siddique (radhiallahu anhu) accompanied Rasulullah (sallallahu alayhi wasallam). On their arrival at Madinah Tayyibah the Ansaar (Helpers or the Sahaabah of Madinah who assisted the Sahaabah of Makkah Mukarramah) came out in crowds to welcome Nabi (sallallahu alayhi wasallam). The Ansaar had not seen Rasulullah (sallallahu alayhi wasallam) as yet, hence on account of Hadhrat Abu Bakr's (radhiallahu anhu) advanced age they mistook him for the Rasool. Under this impression they began making musaafahah with him. It is very significant that Hadhrat Abu Bakr (radhiallahu anhu) did not decline when the people mistakenly shook hands with him. This act of his is indicative of the perfection of his intelligence. He continued making musaafahah with all of them. Since Rasulullah (sallallahu alayhi wasallam) was very tired on account of the arduous journey, Hadhrat Abu Bakr (radhiallahu anhu) did not wish to impose the inconvenience of crowds making musaafahah on Nabi-e-Kareem (sallallahu alayhi wasallam). By substituting himself, Hadhrat Abu Bakr (radhiallahu anhu) saved Rasulullah (sallallahu alayhi wasallam) from considerable inconvenience. If someone adopts this method today in the presence of his Shaikh, he will be regarded as a highly disrespectful person and will be severely criticized and reprimanded.

Nowadays external etiquettes of respect are regarded to be service. True service is to ensure the comfort of the one whose service is intended even if one has to undergo inconvenience and difficulty in the process. This is the meaning of muhabbat (love). The Sahaabah practically demonstrated this.

(9) When making musaafahah, take into consideration the pleasure and the comfort of the one with whom you intend to make musaafahah. Refrain from adopting a method which will displease and inconvenience him.

(10) Making musaafahah after Salaat (as is the practice in some places) is bid'ah.

(11) Do not make musaafahah with one who is engrossed in some work. Just as there are rules for Salaam so are there rules for Musaafahah. According to the Hadith Musaafahah is the completion of Salaam.

14

(12) In some places while making musaafahah the thumbs are pressed. It is claimed that in the thumbs are the veins of love. This is baseless and the narration is a fabrication.

AADAAB OF A MAJLIS (GATHERING)

(1) When you have to wait for someone in a gathering, do not sit in such a place or in such a way as to convey that you are waiting. This action will create unnecessary anxiety for the one whom you are waiting for. Sit down quietly at a distance from the person in an inconspicuous way. (An emergency or urgency will obviously be excluded from this rule)

(2) When going to meet a person then on arrival notify him in some way of your presence. Such notification may be by Salaam, speech or by sitting down (in a gathering) where you may be observed. (This rule does not apply to a public gathering, e.g. a public lecture in a Musjid or other public venue.) Without having informed the person concerned of your arrival do not sit down in such a place which conceals your presence. It is quite possible that he may engage in some conversation which is not meant for your ears. In this way the private affairs of another person may be unwittingly overheard. It is not permissible to overhear the secrets and private affairs of others without their consent. On such occasions if it transpires that someone is engaging in a private conversation without having knowledge of your presence, then immediately leave the place. If this happens while the speaker is under the impression that you are asleep, then immediately reveal that you are not asleep. If the matter being discussed pertains to the infliction of harm or loss to you or to any Muslim, then it will be permissible to overhear such schemes and plots to enable you to protect yourself.

(3) When sitting in the company of a person do not sit in such close proximity as to cause inconvenience to him nor sit so far away that it becomes difficult to conduct the conversation with ease.

(4) Don't sit staring at a person who is involved in some work. This distracts his attention and disturbs his peace.

(5) It is disrespectful to unnecessarily sit directly behind someone in close proximity. The person in front is disturbed thereby.

(6) When someone is sitting and engaged in some work do not stand in his presence waiting for him to attend to you. Sit down and address him as soon as he is relieved of the work.

(7) When going to meet a person do not sit with him so long as to inconvenience him or to cause an impediment in his work.

(8) Where people are gathered do not spit or clean your nose in their presence unnecessarily. For such acts leave their presence.

15

(9) When leaving a gathering which was organized to discuss certain issues, do not leave without the consent of the leader of the assembly.

(10) It is not permissible to remain in a gathering where any law of the Shariat is being violated. Participating in such a gathering is not lawful.

(11) Hadhrat Jaabir (radhiallahu anhu) narrates that Rasulullah (sallallahu alayhi wasallam) said that gatherings are held in trust. It is therefore not permissible to publicize the discussion of the gathering. However, according to the Hadith if th e gathering is a conspiracy to destroy the life, property or reputation of a Muslim, then it will not be permissible to conceal such a plot. If by publicizing the private discussion of the gathering some harm will be caused to a person then such an act will be sinful. If the harm concerns the general public then to a greater extent will it be sinful to advertise or reveal the talks of the private gathering.

(12) While the talk in a gathering is in progress, the newcomer who enters should not make Salaam or Musaafahah. So doing is an interference which disturbs the speaker and distracts the attention of the audience.

(13) When arriving at a gathering early, sit in front. Latecomers should sit at the back wherever they are able to find place. They should not attempt to force their way to the front. Some people arriving late on Fridays at the Musjid, penetrate the rows ahead of them in their attempts to obtain sitting place infront. Such inconsiderate action has been severely criticized in the Hadith. Rasulullah (sallallahu alayhi wasallam) said that such a person will be transformed into a bridge of Jahannum to be trampled on by people. The practice of cutting through the musallis in order to reach the front rows in the Musjid contains four severe evils:
Causing hurt to a Muslim, pride, despising a Muslim and show. Each one of these is a grave crime from which one should abstain.

(14) Without a valid reason do not lean against the wall when in a gathering listening to a discourse. This is highly disrespectful.

(15) If there is ample sitting place available, do not sit with your back towards anyone.

AADAAB OF SPEECH

(1) Some people do not speak clearly. They speak ambiguously and with formality. They consider the use of indications to be respectful. The listener sometimes does not get the message clearly and sometimes he understands wrongly. This causes much inconvenience. Therefore, speak up and speak clearly, without ambiguity.

(2) Speak from in front of a person, not from behind. Speaking from behind a person is perplexing.

(3) When renewing a request to a person, then mention it fully inspite of it having been stated before. Do not express yourself incompletely or ambiguously relying on an earlier explanation. It is possible that the earlier explanation has been partly forgotten, hence the listener may misunderstand the request if it is renewed without clarity.

(4) Some people sitting at the back in a gathering clear their throats or cough in order to attract attention to themselves. If there is a real need to say something, go to the front and explain. However, this should not be done unnecessarily. It is improper to disturb a person involved in some work. Wait for the person to complete his task then address him.

(5) Until such time that one topic has not been completed do not introduce another. While someone is speaking do not interrupt with another subject.

(6) On making an enquiry reply in full, without ambiguity, when you are questioned. Do not reply with confusing statements which necessitate repeated questioning.

(7) While eating do not mention such things which nauseates or disgusts others. The disposition of some persons is delicate and cannot tolerate to hear the mention of disgusting things while eating.

(8) In the presence of a sick person or his housefolk do not make such statements which causes them grief and to lose hope in life. Make encouraging statements to alleviate the pain and sorrow, Insha'Allah.

(9) If you have to speak privately about a person who happens to be present, do not indicate this to another by means of the sign of the hand or eye. Do not let him realize that you are at all discussing him. This will apply if the discussion regarding him is permissible. If the discussion is not lawful, then discussing him will be sinful.

(10) On hearing news of someone's illness, death, etc., do not publicize it until you have confirmed the truth of the news.

(11) Rasulullah (sallallahu alayhi wasallam) said:
       "Do not speak much besides Thikrullaah.
       Verily, abundant speech hardens the heart and the one with a
       hard heart is furthest from Allah."
This applies to futile speech even though the talk may be lawful.

Imaam Maalik (rahmatullah alayh) narrates that Hadhrat Isaa (alayhis salaam) said:
       "Do not speak in abundance for your heart will be hardened."
In other words, fear and humility will be eliminated from the heart. Experience confirms this fact.

(12) Hadhrat Ali (radhiallahu anhu) said that one should speak to people what they are able to understand. Do not discuss with them things which

17

are beyond their intellectual capacities.   Hadhrat Ali (radhiallahu anhu) added:

"Do you wish them to refute Allah and His Rasool?"

Some people will not hesitate to reject such Deeni narrations which they are unable to comprehend.

Hadhrat Ibn Mas'ood (radhiallahu anhu) said:

"When you mention to people such things which are beyond their intellectual capacities, then such talks will most certainly become a cause for the corruption of some people."

(13) Do not unnecessarily adopt the speech styles and slang of those who are ignorant of the Deen.

(14) Be moderate in speech. Do not expand the discussion so much that people become tired and perplexed nor abbreviate the talk to such an extent that the aim and object of the discussion are not understood.

(15) A female should exercise care when speaking. She should not allow her voice to be heard by men unnecessarily.

In like manner a man should not express himself sentimentally in the presence of females. It is obligatory that a man abstains from reciting poetry and expressing himself melodiously in front of females. (i.e. such females for whom the Shar'i law of Hijaab applies).

(16) Do not mumble when speaking. Speak with clarity.

(17) Be to the point. Do not beat about the bush when speaking.

(18) Think before speaking. Sometimes a wrong statement uttered without thinking leads one to Jahannum. One will obtain salvation from this calamity, by inculcating the habit of thinking before speaking.

(19) Do not insult anyone. Do not say to anyone:

`Faasiq, kaafir, mal'oon (cursed), the enemy of Allah.'

(20) Do not be two-tongued, expressing views in the presence of a person calculated to please him, but when in the company of one holding another view, then speaking to please him.

(21) Never engage in gossip, slander and scandalising.

However, it will be permissible to speak contrary to fact and reality in order to restore peace and good relationship between antagonists or enemies.

(22) Do not flatter anyone.

(23) Do not become embroiled with anyone in obstinate debate and argument. When you realize that the person is not prepared to accept the

18

truth, maintain silence. Do not become intransigent and bigoted. Bigotry is exceptionally evil.

(24) Abstain from statements in which there is neither Deeni benefit nor worldly benefit.

(25) Do not curse or speak ill of time (the age). Time is blameless. By implication the criticism is directed to Allah Ta'ala, Nauthubillaah!

(26) Do not praise those who are not upholders of the Deen. (Abstention from praising them should not be construed to mean permissibility to hold them in contempt. It is not permissible to despise them nor to adopt a holier than thou attitude.)

(27) It is haraam to speak ill (gheebat) of even children, insane persons and non-Muslims.

(28) To deliberately listen to gheebat being spoken is as if one has made gheebat.

(29) Juniors should not call their seniors by their names. They should adopt a name or title of respect and honour.

(30) When meeting someone casually, e.g. along the road or by chance, do not engage in a topic which you will not be able to complete in the short while you are with him. If by the time of separating, the topic has not been concluded, you will either waste your time to complete the story or you will depart with the story unfinished. This leaves the listener in suspense and doubt.

(31) If a person mistakes you for another, then immediately rectify him and state your identity.

(32) In the presence of others do not use such terms which are considered uncultural. Express yourself in a cultured way, e.g. say 'the call of nature', etc.

(33) Where the company consists of three persons, two should not speak by whispering to each other, nor should they ask the third one to leave, nor should they speak in a language which the third person does not understand. This causes distress to him.

(34) While two persons are speaking, a third one should not interrupt nor should he present his views unless asked to do so.

(35) When someone is about to relate an incident to you, then even if you are aware of it do not silence him by saying that you know about it. With the intention of pleasing him listen to his talk.

(36) When someone speaks ill of your seniors, do not inform them thereof. Informing them will cause grief to them.

(37) Do not camouflage your error, giving it an interpretation to avoid the error being known. Acknowledge the error and offer an apology. Even acknowledging one's errors fifty times does not appear as bad as offering a devious interpretation once.

(38) Do not indulge in story-telling unnecessarily. Do not waste the time of a busy person by prolonging the conversation with small talk.

(39) Do not answer unnecessary objections. When you discern that the objector's motive is only to object, not to learn or understand the truth, maintain silence or tell him:
"Go! You have understood it so."

(40) On obtaining the answer for your question, do not maintain silence. If you have understood the answer, declare it in some way. If you have not understood, then ask for clarification.

(41) Most people suffer from the malady of stating their case incompletely. This causes great perplexity. State your case fully.

(42) Even on entering your own home, announce your arrival. Enter with consent. One does not know in which condition the womenfolk in the home may be or maybe a *na-mahram* female is present. (Na-mahram female is a woman for whom hijaab is incumbent.) Entering without permission is uncouth and uncultural.

(43) Rasulullah (sallallahu alayhi wasallam) said that among the rights of a Mu'min is that he be addressed with respect and affection. The prevalent custom among the Arabs (during the early times) was to address people by their family name. Rasulullah (sallallahu alayhi wasallam) himself called Hadhrat Abu Bakr (radhiallahu anhu) by the title, `Ateeq'; Hadhrat Umar (radhiallahu anhu) by the title, `Farooq'; Hadhrat Humzah (radhiallahu anhu) by the title `Asadullaah' and Hadhrat Khalid Bin Waleed (radhiallahu anhu) by the title, `Saifuliaah'.

(44) When meeting a person for the first time introduce yourself sufficiently. Provide your name and place of residence (town or country).

(45) Speak the truth, but not harshly and unculturally. Declare the truth respectfully and in soft words. Do not speak in such terms calculated to hurt the feelings of others.

(46) Do not speak regarding a matter which you have not confirmed.

(47) Do not speak sarcastically.

(48) Do not crack such jokes which are hurting to others nor speak in a way which embarrasses people.

(49) Do not call people by detestable nicknames. Nicknames which are hurting or which proclaim some defect in a person fall within the category of gheebat (gheebat means to mention such a truth about a person which he dislikes. Thus gheebat is a true statement about a person, which he detests or which hurts him. If the statement is false, it will be known as buhtaan (slander). About gheebat Rasulullah (sallallahu alayhi wasallam) said: "Gheebat is worse than fornication." The evil and sin of buhtaan are worse.)

(50) Do not speak mockingly of anyone.

(51) Do not speak on the basis of mere suspicion. While you are entitled to safeguard yourself on the basis of suspicion, it is not permissible to blame someone or accuse on the basis of suspicion.

SOME MALFOOZAAT (SAYINGS, STATEMENTS, ADVICES AND ADMONITION) OF HAKIMUL UMMAT HADHRAT MAULANA ASHRAF ALI THAANVI (rahmatullah alayh)

(1)   Some people do not speak clearly. They regard formality and ceremonial expressions and speaking in ambiguous terms as respect and honour. Sometimes the listener does not fully understand the purport of what is being said. This causes immediate perplexity. Therefore, proclaim your case very clearly.

(2)   On enquiring from a newcomer of his time of departure, he (the newcomer) replied: "When you command." Hadhrat Thaanvi (rahmatullah alayh) then educated him in the following manner:

> "What can I understand of your condition from a meaningless answer? What do I know of the time at your disposal. In your reply you should have expressed your intention If you indeed subscribe to this degree of respect, obedience and submission, then after having informed of your intention you should say: `This is my intention, but I leave it to your order.' Do not reply in a manner which is perplexing."

(3) Hadhrat Thaanvi (rahmatullah alayh) enquired about the whereabouts of a worker from a student (who was studying at the Madrasah of Hadhrat Thaanvi). The student said that the worker was sleeping. Afterwards it was established that the worker was awake in his room. The student was admonished in the following manner:

> "Firstly, it is wrong to make a categoric statement on the basis of an assumption. If you were speaking on the basis of an assumption, you should have mentioned this. You should have said: `Perhaps he is asleep.' This is the most that may be said.  However, the actual and proper reply should have been: `I do not know. I shall go and find out.' Then, after having investigated, the correct information should be furnished.

> Secondly, I consider it a merciless act to unnecessarily awaken a sleeping person. Thus, under this impression that he is sleeping and because I loathe disturbing a resting person, I would have tolerated some harm or loss in some wor'· (which had to be executed by the worker). But, when later it transpired that he was not sleeping, it would have caused me unpleasantness. At the same time I would be angry with the informer. All this annoyance is the consequence of speaking without investigation. Always bear this in mind."

(4) On the arrival of a man, Hadhrat asked: "What has brought you? Do you wish to say something?" In reply, the man said: 'I have come only to meet you.'

After the Maghrib Fardh (before even performing the Sunnats) he requested a Ta'weez. Hadhrat Thaanvi commented:

"There is a time and a place for everything. This is not the time for Ta'weez. When you had arrived, I specifically asked you if you have any need. You said that you merely came for mulaaqaat (to greet). Now, what is the meaning of this request at this time? You had immediately to make your request when I had asked. People consider such an attitude (as was adopted by the man) as respect, but I regard it as being highly disrespectful. It (your attitude) implies that others are your servants. Service may thus be taken from them at whim and fancy. You yourself reflect a bit. I have many duties to attend to now. The Sunnats and the Nafl Salaat have yet to be performed. I have to address some Thaakireen and Shaaghileen (those who are engaged in Thikrullaah and spiritual devotional exercises). I have to hear to their requests. I have to see to the feeding of the guests. Alas! In our time respect and culture have totally been effaced from this world. You can come again some other time for a Ta'weez. Remember! Wherever you go, first state your purpose, especially when you are asked. In fact, on the arrival of a person I immediately enquire the purpose of the visit so that he may say whatever he wishes to. This saves him from inconvenience and it saves me from inconvenience.

"I generally ask for the purpose of the visit because most people who come have some need or the other. Some are bashful and are unable to express themselves freely in a gathering. They are not able to reveal a private matter in the gathering. On asking them, they will indicate that they wish to say something in private. When I find the opportunity I call them in privacy and give them audience. But when a person does not open his mouth, how can I understand? I do not possess knowledge of the ghaib (unseen things)."

(5) One student, while Hadhrat was involved in Ta'leem (teaching those present) and before the termination of the talk, commenced to explain a dream which he had seen. Hadhrat Thaanvi said:

"What is this act? Before one topic has ended, you interrupt with another. The talk of an intelligent man has a beginning and an ending. Don't interrupt a discussion with another topic. An intelligent man will not speak while another is involved in discussion. Your interruption implies that the aim is to explain a dream. Ta'leem (teaching) and Talqeen (instruction) are futile to you. In otherwords, my lengthy talk is worthless. In future never repeat this mistake. Now

23

get up and leave. The meaning (of your dream) will be explained at some other time. Presently you have dishonoured Ta'leem."

(6) Hadhrat Thaanvi said:

"I detest stories and narrations. People squander my time with futile talks. Sometimes, out of politeness, I say nothing. One should involve in useful things."

(7) A man came to Hadhrat Thaanvi with some salt for the purpose of reciting on it. (This is a valid and permissible act. As a result of the blessing of the recitation of the Qur'aanic words, the substance on which the recital is directed acquires healing properties). However, the man did not explain his case fully and clearly. Hadhrat, therefore, commented:

"When you have stated your case fully, then only will I recite."

Directing his attention to the gathering, Hadhrat said:

"It comes in the Hadith that once a man entered in the presence of Rasulullah (sallallahu alayhi wasallam) without having obtained permission. Rasulullah (sallallahu alayhi wasallam) ordered him to leave. At the same time Rasulullah (sallallahu alayhi wasallam) instructed one person to teach him the correct etiquette of seeking permission before entering. This establishes that practical instruction is Sunnat. People with dense minds cannot remember without practical demonstration."

(8) Once Hadhrat commented:

"I become highly perplexed with vexing talks. I wish statements to be clear, without ambiguity. I state a matter with clarity and I expect others to do likewise. But, most people lack the habit of speaking clearly."

(9) A newcomer on arrival, after making musafahah (shaking hands) presented another person's letter, saying that a certain man had sent this letter. Hadhrat said:

"You should firstly introduce yourself. I have not recognized you. You should give priority first to yourself, then be concerned about others (in such matters)."

The newcomer replied: "I am a student studying in a certain Madrasah" (he mentioned the name of the Madrasah). Saying this much, he remained silent. After a brief pause, Hadhrat said:

"By saying this much, you consider it sufficient introduction."

The newcomer again remained silent. Once again hadhrat asked:

"You have no name nor hometown?"

The student again remained silent. Hadhrat then commented:

"I have no remedy for this. Even after I have complained, he has not introduced himself. If my asking and questioning seem futile and unintelligent to you, then get up and sit over there (at a distance). It is futile for you to sit near to me."

(10) A newcomer remained silent after Hadhrat enquired about his hometown and the purpose of his visit. Hadhrat commented:
"Brother! Say whatever you wish to. At least introduce yourself so that I may know the purpose of your long journey and the reason why you have spent so much time and money. What is your purpose? How can another person know what is in your mind without you speaking? There is no *Ilm-e-ghaib* (knowledge of the unseen) here by which the purpose of your leaving and undertaking this journey may be known. After all, you must be having some purpose and motive. State it clearly. What intricacy is involved in stating your aim."

Even after this admonition, the newcomer maintained silence, not saying anything. Hadhrat said:
"No one considers these acts (of perplexity) of those who come here. They do not see what these people are doing. But, they complain when I admonish them. This is just as a person silently pricking another with a needle. When the injured person exclaims in pain and agony, all hear it while no one sees the cause of the exclamation and screaming. People have heard the name of *Islaah* (self-reformation) but they are totally ignorant of the meaning and reality of *Islaah*. A man becomes a true man only after great difficulty and striving."

(11) A man, on presenting a letter attempted to engage in a verbal discussion. Hadhrat said:
"Why this confusion? A letter as well as a verbal discussion! Either you should have stated your whole case verbally or in writing. If for some reason you wished to do both, then the correct method is to first state the matter verbally and then only mention the letter. Now by simultaneously combining both, I am perplexed for I do not know if the subject in the letter is the same or different from what is said verbally. Such acts bring about unnecessary perplexity and concern. But, they do not discern this although others are inconvenienced. I do not understand whether the whole world is filled with people of bad understanding or such persons have been ordained as my share after they have been picked out from the rest (of mankind). What was the wisdom in presenting the letter and simultaneously commencing a verbal discussion?"

The man expressed his profound apologies after acknowledging his error.

(12) Admonishing a man who made a statement without having investigated the matter, Hadhrat said:

25

"How could you have made this statement without having made an investigation? It appears as if you are suffering from the malady of speaking much, hence without investigating the incident you commenced blabbing. When this is the condition of such cultured people (as yourself), then what complaint can one have of others?"

(13) In reply to a question by one Molvi Saheb, Hadhrat said:
"Inspite of having acquired so much education you do not know the etiquette and way of questioning. You have learnt the Kitaabs merely in parrot fashion. If you had studied the Kitaabs with understanding, you would not have posed your question in such an uncultured manner. I have been severely disturbed by this manner of your questioning. Afterall, what constrains you people to be so careless? You speak without thinking. Whatever comes on your tongue, you proclaim it. When this is your condition, then what can we say about the poor laity?"

The Molvi Saheb replied:
"Truly, I have erred. Insha'Allah, in future it will not happen. I shall take care. Forgive me."

Hadhrat further commented:
"Alas! Your condition is extremely regrettable. To what extent should I maintain sabr (patience)? If I admonish and draw attention to such errors of speech, I stand ciriticized. If I maintain silence and do not admonish you, you will become (spiritually and morally) corrupted. Anyhow, you have promised to exercise care in the future. It is best that you now again pose your question so that I may see if you do not repeat your error."

The Molvi Saheb repeated his question and Hadhrat commented:
"Now it is correct. Look! With slight reflection the question has been corrected. I always maintain that in most cases the cause underlying errors is not bad understanding, but is carelessness. The present case testifies that if the question (which the Molvi Saheb had made at first) was the result of bad understanding, then how did he manage to correct it so quickly? On having reflected, he corrected the error."

(14) Admonishing a man on an error, Hadhrat said:
"Why did you not state your case fully? What were you afterall waiting for? You ventured an answer only after being questioned and that too, incomplete."

He replied: "Hadhrat you were busy writing."

26

Hadhrat commented: "Did I have to discontinue writing on account of your presence. Do I possess knowledge of the unseen by which I may know that a certain person has arrived and he has something to say? Why have you spoken now? Now too I am busy writing. You people resort to meaningless interpretations. Why do you trouble yourselves as well as others? Even now you have not spoken correctly nor replied correctly. Even now you have repeated the same perplexing statement. What harm will I suffer? I have diagnosed your pulses. When your condition is such that you conceal your faults and errors, then what hope is there for your reformation? Afterall, what is the reason underlying the concealment of maladies? I fully understand it. I am involved in this activity for a long time now. Let me inform you of the sickness."

The man said: "Hadhrat, now forgive me. In future I will be more careful. Truly, I have erred."

Hadhrat commented: "You are forgiven, but the malady in you will not be cured by forgiveness. The malady is *jaah* (the love for fame). This causes concealment of faults. Treat it. If you do not, then remember you will lose whatever you have gained (spiritually and morally). I desire that maladies be cured with ease. But, you people choose difficulty. I have no remedy for that."

(15) Admonishing a newcomer, Hadhrat said:
"Neither can you state your case nor can you understand the next man. Under the circumstances it is futile to converse with you. When you cannot even introduce yourself, speaking futile things, then what hope is there that you will act correctly in future? I do not wish to strike up an association with such a person. Now get up and leave."

Thereupon the newcomer fully introduced himself. Hadhrat then commented:
"From whence did you obtain the understanding so quickly? It is but what I am always saying, viz., people suffer from the disease of carelessness. Now when concern asserted itself, the mind and the heart began operating and executing their functions. Without a whip the horse will not work."

(16) A rural dweller came and said: "Hazratji give me a ta'weez." Hadhrat said: "I have not understood." The man exclaimed loudly: "Give me a ta'weez." Hadhrat replied: "I am not deaf. I have heard you, but I have not understood you." The man remained silent. Hadhrat commented: "Now you sit as if you are dumb. Why do you not state your case fully? Have you taken an oath at home that you will come and trouble me?" He said: "How should I say?" Hadhrat said:

"Go outside and enquire from someone, then come. Inform (whoever you ask) that I have said this." He left and after enquiring from someone he returned and said:

"Yes, my statement was incomplete."

On this occasion he stated the type of ta'weez he required. Hadhrat commented: "This villager never went to the station and said: `Give me a ticket.' He never refrained from asking for a ticket to proceed to a specific place. Similarly he never went to the bazaar to purchase something without clearly stating the product he required. It seems that all ignorance has been ordained as my lot. What! Is it death for you to state your full case?"

The man said: "We are village-dwellers. Our understanding is such."
Hadhrat commented: "You people are very clever.
Now since your understanding is such, go and return after an hour for the ta'weez. When you come, state clearly your request. Do not rely on what you have already asked (i.e. the type of ta'weez). I will not remember afterwards."

After an hour he returned and expressed himself fully and satisfactorily. He then left with the ta'weez. Hadhrat commented:

"He will never forget this lesson. He will henceforth speak fully even if he goes elsewhere. If I don't adopt this method, ignorance will not be dispelled."

THE AADAAB OF LISTENING TO TALK

(1) Listen attentively. If any part of the talk is not clear or a doubt lingers, seek its clarification from the speaker immediately. Don't act on what has been said on the basis of your opinion.

(2) When someone calls you, reply immediately so that the caller knows that you have heard him.

(3) When someone speaks to you, do not listen with indifference. This attitude will hurt his feelings. This applies to a greater extent when someone speaks for your benefit or answers your question.

(4) When someone assigns a task to you, express your intention verbally. Say yes or no, etc. Perhaps you have no intention of doing the work and by your silence the speaker gains the impression that you have agreed to undertake the task.

(5) When someone speaks ill of your Ustaadh, then remain silent. If it becomes unbearable, leave the place.

(6) When your Ustaadh speaks, apply your whole attention to him.

(7) After having attentively listened to your Ustaadh's discourse, if you do not understand anything, do not attribute it to your Ustaadh. On the contrary, regard your inability as a result of your defective understanding and inattentiveness.

(8) It is not permissible to listen to music and singing. The heart is corrupted thereby. Evil dominates the nafs. Music gives impetus to the evil qualities of the lowly nafs. The inclination to commit wrong is thus stirred in man. Whatever leads to haraam is likewise haraam.

(9) Avoid listening to the voices of females and young boys. A woman should exercise caution in this regard. She should ensure that her voice does not reach the ears of *ghair mahram* males (i.e. males for whom hijaab is compulsory).

(10) Do not get up and leave while someone is addressing you. This will hurt the feelings of the speaker, and will exhibit your unappreciativeness of the talk. (This applies to lawful talk. If the talk is not lawful, then it will not be permissible to listen to it.)

(11) When listening to a lecture, do not engage in any other conversation. Pay attention to the discourse. It is disrespectful to engage in a conversation at such a time and it displays lack of appreciation of the discourse.

(12) When someone calls you from behind a partition, etc., reply immediately to put the caller at ease. Do not remain silent, for then the caller will persist in calling.

(13) When some_ne assigns a duty to you, listen to it well and after having executed it, notify him of its accomplishment. This will avoid suspense and anticipation.

(14) If you have not understood, say so. Do not pretend that you have understood. Do not say, `yes, yes'.

(15) On announcing yourself, e.g. by having made Salaam, if the inmates of the house have not recognized you and they ask, `Who is it?, do not say: `It's me.' State your name.

(16) It is highly disrespectful to remain silent after having heard the question. Similarly, it is disrespectful and cause for much annoyance to reply after some delay.

SOME MALFOOZAAT OF HADHRAT MAULANA
ASHRAF AU THAANVI (rahmatullah alayh)
PERTAINING TO LISTENING

(1) Hadhrat Thaanvi had granted a certain Thaakir (one who passes his time in Thikrullaah) some time for discussion after Maghrib at his request. After Maghrib, Hadhrat called him because he was seated at a distance. Although the Thaakir started to come towards Hadhrat, he did not answer the call to indicate that he had heard it. But, Hadhrat was not apprized of his coming, hence he called a second time. Meanwhile the Thaakir had arrived. Hadhrat asked:

"Why did you not answer? By answering, the caller will know that the one who has been called has heard the call. By not replying, there is uncertainty and this necessitates repeated calling. This inconvenience is the result purely of your negligent attitude. What difficulty was there in saying, `Yes!'? Nowadays, academic knowledge is imparted in every place. But, there is a dearth of Akhlaaq (moral character). Now I have been annoyed and perplexed. I will give you another time. Remember this."

(2) A man presented a paper to Hadhrat who wrote a ta'weez and explained its method. After having heard the method of the ta'weez, he remained silent. He did not say whether he had understood or not. Hadhrat asked: "Have you understood the method explained by me?"

The man said: "I have heard it." Hadhrat said: "Then why do you not say, yes or no?" He replied: "My hearing is not good." Hadhrat said: "You said that you have understood the method. In otherwords, you said that you have understood it without having heard it. In the beginning you should have said you cannot hear properly. Answer me. Have you understood what I have said?" He replied: 'I have understood a bit.' Hadhrat said: "You should have answered and informed of whatever you have understood. By answering, the other person will be relieved." The man said: "I have erred." Hadhrat commented: "Do not repeat again such an error." Thereupon, addressing the gathering, Hadhrat said: "It is not the fault of these poor people. It is the fault of the elders who refrain from admonition."

AADAAB OF MULAAQAAT (MEETING ONE ANOTHER)

(1) When you go to meet a person do not disturb him by intruding while he is busy. If for example, he is engaged in Tilaawat, Wazeefah or he is in privacy or sleeping or preparing to sleep or involved in something else in which he will be disturbed if you intrude or he may be inconvenienced by your intrusion, then at such a time do not greet or shake hands. Either go away and return later or wait elsewhere (where his attention will not be attracted). If the matter is urgent and requires immediate attention, seek his permission first.

(2) When having arrived at the venue of the person whom you wish to meet, inform him of your presence either by Salaam, speech, etc. Do not sit in a concealed place or in such a way that he has not learnt of your presence. Perhaps he wishes to say something which is not intended for your ears. It is evil to listen in to another person's secrets without his consent. If you realize that the discussion in progress is not for your ears, immediately take leave.

(3) When meeting someone with whom you have no informal association, do not ask him about the condition of his home affairs. Similarly, do not ask him about his source of earning, possessions, etc.

(4) On meeting a person do not linger too long so as to cause him inconvenience or to constitute an impediment in his activity.

(5) When meeting someone, do so pleasantly and smilingly so as to please him.

(6) When meeting someone for the first time, remember the following things:

* Introduce yourself. State your name.
* State your hometown or the country or city from where you are coming.
* State the purpose of your visit.

(7) When meeting a person, do not pick up any letter, paper or book from nearby to read.

(8) When someone comes to meet you (and if you are sitting) get up or move slightly. In this is respect for the visitor.

SOME MALFOOZAAT

(1) A newcomer entered, made musaafahah and departed without saying anything. Hadhrat commented:

> "Is this also some form of humanity? He pleased himself and disturbed the heart of others. When a stranger comes it is only natural to wonder who he is, from where he has come, for what purpose has he come. Has he thought me to be an idol, merely putting his hands in my hands and moving off as if I am lifeless. These are natural things (which do not require instruction)".

(2) Some people commit the error of arriving without notifying. They have not yet eaten, but arrive at such a time which creates difficulty in preparing food. If it is realized that the time of arrival will be improper, then make your own food arrangements. After having eaten, proceed to meet the person, and on reaching there inform him that you have already made your food arrangements so that he does not labour in suspense and uncertainty.

(3) One should not wait in expectation of being asked to introduce oneself. At the first available opportunity introduce yourself. At the time of greeting, make your introduction and state your purpose. It is necessary for the host to make himself available for this purpose. At the time of meeting, he should leave off his activity.

THE AADAAB OF THE GUEST

(1) The Guest should immediately notify the host if he has no intention of eating there for some reason or the other. It should not happen that the host prepares food and then all goes to waste. This will cause much grief to the host who underwent inconvenience and laboured to make hospitable arrangements for the guest.

(2) The guest should inform the host of his whereabouts so that the latter (host) does not have to search for him when meals are ready to be served.

(3) The guest should not accept anyone's invitation without the consent of the host.

(4) The guest should not interfere in the arrangements and system of the host. However, there is nothing wrong if the host assigns an arrangement or an act to the guest.

(5) The guest should never adopt a demanding attitude or tone. He should tender his wishes with humble request.

33

(6) If the guest is on a diet, he should inform his host immediately on arrival. Some persons exhibit ill-manners in this regard at the exact time of eating when the food has been served.

(7) The guest should not ask the host for something, for perhaps the host is unable to fulfil the request and is thus put to shame. (Necessities are excluded.)

(8) The guest should leave a little food over so that the host does not think that maybe the food was not enough and the guest has not eaten sufficiently. This will put the host to shame. (This does not mean that the guest should leave some of the food in his plate uneaten. He should clean, the plate with his fingers. This is Sunnat. Some food should, however, be left in the serving utensils.)

(9) Do not accompany an invited person to his host's residence. The host, merely out of shame may be constrained to ask you to remain for meals while in actual fact he has no intention of doing so. This causes difficulty to the host. Some persons very quickly accept such instant invitations which are made by coincidence. The host may feel belittled if he does not ask you to remain for meals.

(10) Do not inconvenience the host nor put him to shame by making a request at the time of departure. The time for fulfilling your request may be too less and the host will suffer shame by not being able to satisfy the guest.

(11) If several varieties of food are served, the guest should taste a bit of every variety. This is a right which the host has over the guest. However, if the guest is ill or on a prescribed medical diet, then this will be an exception.

(12) Do not initiate an intricate topic while eating. The talk should be light, otherwise the pleasure of the food will be destroyed. While eating, the greater part of one's attention should be directed to the food.

(13) It is not permissible for a guest to give any food to a beggar or anyone else (i.e. from the food which the host has served). Similarly, if some food is presented in a utensil, it is not permissible to eat from the utensil. Remove the food into own utensil. However, if the form of the food will be destroyed by emptying it in another utensil, then it will be permissible to eat from the utensil in which it was sent, e.g. pudding.

(14) When going to a place for some work, etc. and while there you go to meet an acquaintance, then immediately inform him of your staying arrangements so that he does not gain the impression that you are his guest.

(15) The Ulama should be extremely careful when going to eat at the place of their host. They should not impose on the hospitality of the host by taking along with them a group of friends/students/mureeds.

MALFOOZAAT

(1) A student came as a guest to Hadhrat Thaanvi (rahmatullah alayh). He had come once before, but had stayed elsewhere. While he intended to stay over here this time, he did not make this known. Thus, food was not sent to him. Afterwards, when he was asked, it transpired that he intended to stay here (at the Khaanqah of Hadhrat). Meals were then sent. Hadhrat advised him as follows:

"When you intend staying, you should make this known yourself. How can one know of your intention if you do not state it?
Since you had stayed elsewhere the previous time, how could you conclude that you would be asked of your intentions?"

(2) Guests have no relationship with futile talk. One guest to another: 'Meals are ready.' He had no right to say this.

(3) A guest asked water from the servant of his host in a demanding tone. Hadhrat commented: "Never adopt a commanding tone. This is bad character. Say: `Please give me some water.'

(4) Once after Isha, a certain person (who was staying as a guest at the Khaanqah) said: I shall go to a certain place to fetch a blanket.' It was said to him that the gates of the Madrasah have already closed, and if he calls for the gate to be opened up, he will be disturbing those who are resting. Someone gave him a blanket. Alas! was he sleeping the whole day? Why did he not make his arrangement earlier.

(5) **OUR CONDUCT**

Nowadays our conduct is of a new kind. It is considered contrary to culture to ask the guest of the duration of his stay. Some guests make their own food arrangement without informing the host. The host undergoes much difficulty to prepare meals for guests and to make them comfortable, but just when meals are about to be served, they inform the host of their own arrangement. The host will suffer considerable grief by this rebuff. A guest who was here brought along his own food but did not inform me. At the time when meals were about to be served, he opened up his food. I said to him: You should have informed me that you had brought food with you. There is nothing wrong in this. Since you did not inform me and imposed a difficulty on me, take this food and sit elsewhere to eat. Do not sit to eat it here.

When I go on a journey and intend to stay over in Saharanpur for a while, and if my arrival coincides with meal-time, I immediately inform on arrival of my intention that : have brought along food or I have arranged to eat at a certain place. If I had taken along some food, then on arrival I will immediately hand it over to the host who can decide what to do with it.

(6) Hadhrat said to a mureed:

"If you have to come on a Friday, bring along your food. If you come some other day, then if possible we may entertain you. We have announced to all that whoever comes on a Friday is not our guest. He has come for Salaatul Juma'h. Furthermore, on Fridays numerous people come from nearby towns (for Juma'h). I do not operate a feasting-house here. Eat at home, then set out. However, those who have journeyed from distant places intending to be my guests, they may arrive any day. They are my guests."

(7) Wherever Maulana Muzaffar Husain (rahmatullah alayh) would go, he would immediately inform: "I shall be your guest for one day or two days." One day this saint was the guest of Hadhrat Maulana Gangohi (rahmatullah alayh). In the morning Maulana Gangohi asked Maulana (the guest) to have breakfast. Maulana Muzaffar had to go to Rampur that morning, and fearing a delay, he said to Maulana Gangohi:

"If you have anything left over from last night's food, bring it."

Maulana Gangohi brought the simple food (which was left over of the previous night) and some stale bread. Maulana Muzaffar Husain took the food along and departed. On reaching Rampur, Maulana Muzaffar Husain spoke highly of Maulana Gangohi in the presence of Hakeem Ziyauddin. Hakeem Saheb commented:

"He is a saint." Maulana Muzaffar Husain said: "I am not praising his sainthood. I am saying that he is a good man. If you don't understand, then ask." Hakeem Saheb said: Hadhrat, inform me." Maulana Muzaffar Husain said: "Look, what a good man he is. He asked me for meals, but on my request, he brought, without any qualms, whatever leftovers he had. For this reason I said that he is a good man."

(8) Once Hadhrat Maulana Gangohi (rahmatullah alayh) was the guest of Hakeem Mueenuddin, the son of Hadhrat Maulana Muhammad Ya'qoob (rahmatullah alayh). The host is very informal type of a person. On that particular day there was no food in the house to serve. The host said:

"Today there is no food by us. However, most friends are eagerly inviting you. If you agree, I can accept an invitation."

Maulana Gangohi replied: "I am your guest and will remain in the condition in which you are." Thus, they remained without food.

THE AADAAB OF THE HOST

(1) The host should not insist that the guest eats. This is contrary to the well-being of the guest.

(2) If there is a need to serve more food, do not remove the utensil (in which there is still some food) from the presence of the host. Bring more food in another utensil.

(3) If the intention is to invite some of the associates of one's Buzrug (Shaikh, Ustaadh, etc.) along with the Buzrug, then do not ask the Buzrug to bring them along. It is disrespectful to extract service from him. Take permission from him and do the inviting yourself. The associate should also seek permission from the Buzrug before accepting the invitation.

(4) Be hospitable to the guest and tend to his needs and comfort. Feed him a sumptuous meal (within one's means) at least on one occasion. The guest has a right of three days.

(5) When sending food to the guest, ensure that it is covered.

(6) When the guest is departing, see him off until the door. This is Sunnat.

(7) The host should not overwhelm the guest with his continuous presence. He should leave the guest free. The guest should be left to eat as he pleases.

(8) People sometimes stare at the guest while he is eating, taking note of what and how much he is eating. The guest is irked by this behaviour.

(9) When the guest arrives, show him the toilets so that he is not inconvenienced if he suddenly has to answer the call of nature.

(10) As soon as the guest arrives, make arrangements for his eating. Whatever is easily available and could be prepared quickly should be arranged. If by the means, more sumptuous meals may be arranged later.

(11) Do not go out of your way in acquiring things for the guest. Whatever good things are easily available, make do with them. Do not be unnecessarily formal.

(12) The host should not merely deliver the food to the guest and leave thereafter. He should remain to see to the further needs of the guest. While keeping a watchful eye on the guests, the host should not stare at the guest nor make him aware of his attention. He should merely cast an occasional glance to ascertain whether the guest requires anything more.

(13) When there are two guests, treat them with equality.

MALFOOZAAT

(1) A guest (dhaif) is one who arrives solely on account of friendship. The right (Haqq) of such a guest devolves solely on the person whom the guest came to visit.

A traveller (musaafir or ibnus sabeel) is one who has come for some work or need. In the process he arrives to greet. The right of the musaafir is over all the neighbours (in the locality) in the Kifaayah category, i.e. a single person entertaining the musaafir will suffice to discharge the duty on behalf of the entire neighbourhood.

(2) When I went to Dhaka on the invitation of the Nawaab, Ulama from various parts of Bengal came to meet me. I told all of them to make their own food arrangements. When this reached the ears of the Nawaab he instructed his manager in charge of the food arrangements to notify me that all the Ulama should have their meals at his place. I informed him that they (the Ulama) were my honoured friends. They were not people who merely tagged along with me. I shall not tell them. He should himself invite them if he so wishes and if they accept, it is their pleasure. He then invited them all individually. In this method their respect and esteem were ensured whereas this would not have been the case if they had joined in the eating merely on my account.

(3) Once a bid'ati durwaish (saintly person) was the guest of Hadhrat Maulana Nanotwi (rahmatullah alayh) who honoured the guest considerably. Someone informed Maulana Gangohi (rahmatullah alayh) of this. Maulana Gangohi said that "this was not good". The informer narrated this comment to Maulana Nanotwi who said:

"Rasulullah (sallallahu alayhi wasallam) honoured even kuffaar guests."

This informant conveyed this reply to Maulana Gangohi who commented:

"In honouring a kaafir there is no danger (to Imaan), but in honouring a bid'ati there is danger."

When the informant once again conveyed this comment to Maulana Nanotwi, he reprimanded him and forbade him from carrying messages to and fro.

(4) We should steadfastly adhere to Islamic simplicity. When we desire to be somewhat extravagant in entertaining guests, we should bear in mind the limits of Islamic moderation. Be not wasteful. In observance of moderation is our respect. But, nowadays Muslims regard respect and dignity obtainable in emulating western culture. They emulate western dress, appearance and styles in all facets of life. Truly, there is no respect and honour in such emulation.

(5) Once Imaam Shaafi (rahmatullah alayh) was a guest of a certain person. It was the practice of this host to hand a written menu to the servant who would prepare all the foods listed for the occasion. One day Imaam Shaaf'i took the menu from the slave and added to the list a certain delicacy of which he was very fond. When the host saw the new dish, he enquired from the slave the reason for the additional variety. The slave informed his master that the food was prepared at the request of the guest. This pleased the host so much that in happiness he emancipated the slave.

(6) It is one of my practices to differentiate my guests at meal times. If a number of guests are present I do not gather them all at once to have meals together. If the guests are strangers to one another, I do not feed them together. However, if I join them, then only do I have a single session for meals, for then I act on behalf of them all.

The reason for this practice is that people are of different temperaments, cultural background and persuasions. When strangers are seated together for meals, some people are not able to relax and eat freely and informally. They feel inhibited.

THE AADAAB OF KHIDMAT
(SERVICE TO OTHERS)

(1) Some persons do not prefer accepting service from others. The one who wishes to render service to such persons should not insist on doing so. The one who is served is perplexed and inconvenienced by such service. The attitude of a person can be understood either by his explicit refusal or by some other indication.

(2) Upon accomplishing a duty which someone has requested of you, inform him after it has been done. In most cases, he will be waiting in expectation.

(3) Rendering physical service to one's Shaikh on the first occasion of meeting him is very irksome to him. Should one be eager to render service to the Shaikh, one should first establish an informal and friendly relationship.

(4) While there is comfort in khidmat, there are three conditions to it (khidmat).

* Sincerity: The motive of rendering the service must be nothing other than muhabbat (affection). Most people utilize khidmat as a medium for the attainment of motives.

* Congeniality: The hearts of the khaadim (the one who renders the service) and the makhdoom (the one who is being served) should be at one. There should be congeniality (munasabat) between them. They should not be strangers.

* Ability: The khaadim should know how to render the service he is to undertake.

(5) Service rendered to Muslims in Makkah Muazzamah should be regarded as worship and good fortune provided there is no Shar'i prohibition involved in rendering the service.

(6) Respect and honour people according to their rank.

(7) As far as possible aid a person in need. If you are unable to assist intercede on his behalf so that someone else may render the assistance. However, when interceding first establish whether your intercession will not inconvenience the person.

(8) By assisting orphans one will be blessed with the companionship of Rasulullah (sallallahu alayhi wasallam) in Jannat.

(9) Those who earn and see to the needs of widows and needy relatives, obtain the thawaab of Jihaad.

(10) Aiding the mazloom *(one against whom injustice or oppression is committed)* is very necessary. Sympathy for the zaalim (oppressor) is to prevent him from committing injustices.

(11) The service of giving people water to drink is an act of great thawaab. Rendering this act in a place where water is available in abundance is the equivalent of emancipating a slave. Where water is less, the thawaab of rendering this act is the equivalent of resurrecting to life a dead person.

(12) By assisting someone with insignificant items, e.g. some salt for the food, the thawaab is as if one has prepared the food.

(13) Serve your parents even though they happen to be non-Muslims. Obey parents in all things lawful in the Shariat. (In the process of serving and obeying non-Muslim parents, the laws of the Shariat should not be violated. If, for example, one's non-Muslim father dies and one's mother wishes one to participate in the funeral service, such obedience and service will not be permissible. In short, service and obedience to parents should be within the confines of Islam.)

(14) Meeting with and rendering service to the friends of one's parents after their death are also acts which are regarded in Islam as service to parents.

(15) If one's parents had died while they were displeased with one, then one should always make dua and istighfaar for them. It is hoped that Allah Ta'ala will ensure that they become happy with their children. (Thus the relationship will be restored on the Day of Qiyaamah). Be kind and render service to relatives even though they may be unkind to you.

(16) Service to neighbours occupies a very important place in Islam. Be kind to them. Tolerate their indiscreetness and disturbances. Do not do anything which will upset them or annoy them. If they are in need, tend to them as best as you can.

THE AADAAB OF HADYAH *(GIFT)*

(1) If you wish to make a request to a person for something, then do not make any gift to him. The one to whom the gift is made under such circumstances is either put to disgrace or is indirectly compelled to comply

with the request of the person who presented the gift. (Such a gift will in fact be a bribe).

(2) When taking a gift along the journey to present to someone, do not take so much as to create difficulty for you along the journey.

(3) Immediately after accepting a gift it is not proper to give it (the gift) in charity in the presence of the person who made the gift. Contribute it in the absence of the person in a way which will not be known to him, otherwise he will be grieved.

(4) The motive for making gifts should be only muhabbat (love and affection), not the fulfilment of one's needs or request. Therefore, if you have a need to present to a person, do not make a gift to him at the same time. It will then appear as if the gift was motivated by the ulterior motive.

(5) The actual purpose of making a gift is to strengthen the bond of affection. Therefore, such ways which inconvenience the one for whom the gift is intended, should not be adopted.

(6) Make the gift in privacy, not in public. The *muhda ilayh* (the person to whom the gift was made) is entitled to make public the gift.

(7) If the gift is in kind (i.e. not cash) then endeavour to ascertain the likes and preferences of the *muhda ilayh*. Present something which the muhda ilayh prefers.

(8) The amount of the gift should not be so much that it constitutes a difficulty for the *muhda ilayh*. It does not matter how less or of little value the gift may be. People of piety are not concerned with the amount or quantity of the gift. They look at the sincerity of the one who makes the gift.

(9) If for some reason acceptance of the gift is refused, then respectfully request the reason for the refusal. For the future bear it in mind. But do not insist to obtain the reason at the time. If the gift is refused because of a misunderstanding created by a baseless supposition or misinformation which reached the muhda ilayh, then it is correct, in fact better, to immediately notify him of the error.

(10) Do not make a gift to anyone as long as he is not convinced of your sincerity.

(11) Do not make gifts in such a way that taking delivery of it becomes difficult and onerous on the *muhda ilayh*.

(12) A gift tendered with the motive to obtain some benefit in lieu is, in fact, bribery. It is not hadyah.

(13) If the motive underlying the gift is to obtain thawaab in the Aakhirat, then too, it is not hadyah, but will be Sadqah (charity).

(14) Some people labour under the impression that when going to visit a Saint it is necessary to present a gift to him. This is incorrect. To make it a rule to present him with a gift whenever one visits him is harmful to all parties concerned.

(15) Accept gifts from such persons who do not expect anything in return, otherwise it will lead to ill-feeling ultimately. However, the one who has accepted the gift should endeavour to reciprocate. If you are not by the means to give anything in return, at least praise the person and express your gratitude. Mention his favour in the presence of others. Expressing gratitude by saying
    "May Allah reward your goodness,."
will suffice. One who does not express gratitude to a person who did a favour, does not express gratitude to even Allah Ta'ala.

(16) It is improper to obliterate (i.e. to forget about) a gift which one has received, for this displays lack of appreciation. Similarly, it is improper to advertise with pride the great value or abundance of the gifts received.

(17) It is not permissible to accept gifts from mentally deranged persons.

(18) It is not permissible to accept gifts from na-baaligh (minor) children.

(19) A gift should not be refused because of its slight value or small quantity.

(20) A gift should not be refused on account of pride or arrogance.

(21) If one detects that a gift is not presented because of sincerity, but is motivated by some ulterior motive, then such a gift should be refused.

(22) It is permissible to refuse a gift if one detects that the gift is made or, account of one's need or poverty.

(23) A Qari who has recited the Qur'aan should not be given a present (hadyah) because of his recital. If a gift is made to him, he should refuse acceptance.

(24)   Hadyah (gift) should not be presented while making musaafahah (shaking hands).

(25)   When sending hadyah with someone, ensure that the person whom you are sending is reliable so that there be no need to obtain a receipt or acknowledgement letter from the muhda ilayh (the one to whom the gift is made). Requesting acknowledgement from the *muhda ilayh* is an irksome imposition on him and it is uncultural.

(26)   When a gift is made, the price of the item should not be asked of the one who makes the gift. Similarly, others who happen to be present when the gift is made should also not query the price or value of the article in the presence of the muhdi (the one who makes the gift).

MALFOOZAAT REGARDING HADYAH

(1)   During a journey the people of a certain town had decided to make a collection and present me with a gift on my departure. When I was informed of this, I forbade them. I warned them never to do this. One evil in this method of collecting is that sometimes the donor does not contribute wholeheartedly, but gives as a result of indirect pressure since the collectors may be prominent men of the town. Secondly, the purpose of hadyah is to increase the muhabbat and friendship. Thus, even if the contributor gave wholeheartedly, the aim of the hadyah is lost since the identity of the giver will not be known to the *muhda ilayh*. Thirdly, sometimes it becomes necessary to refuse the gift because of some valid reason. This reason is related to the muhdi (giver). But, in view of his identity being unknown, this becomes difficult because of the collective hadyah. Therefore, whoever wishes to present a gift, should do so himself or without having been exhorted, he should send it with some reliable person. Alternatively, an accompanying letter may be sent with the gift.

(2)   During one journey some persons, taking me to their homes attempted to present hadyah to me. I prevented them from this. I advised them that if others come to know of this, they may gain the impression that it is customary to present gifts in this way. Those who are unable to afford will be put to anxiety when they call me to their homes. They will not know whether they should call me or not. If they do, they will not be able to present gifts and if they do not call me, they will be left with regret. Whoever wishes to make a gift should come to my place of residence, talk with me so that my liberty is not curtailed.

(3)   When some people present gifts to me it appears to me that either it is onerous on them or onerous on me. I feel like refusing such gifts. However,

44

since it is in conflict with the Sunnah to refuse gifts, I used to be bothered about this. But, I obtained clarification in this regard from one Hadith. Rasulullah (sallallahu alayhi wasallam) said that when a pillow or perfume is presented, accept it. Rasulullah (sallallahu alayhi wasallam) stated the reason for this acceptance in the following terms:

"For verily, it is light in weight."
This implies that if a gift is onerous on one's disposition, it may be refused.

(4) Once a great Aalim and Aarif raised the query of accepting gifts after having anticipated them. He said:

"Sometimes when seeing certain sincere friends who usually present gifts, the thought arises in the mind that perhaps they will give hadyah. Then, it just happens that they make gifts. On such occasions there is some trepidation in the heart since this form of hadyah is known as *Ishraafun Nafs*. In the state of *Ishraafun Nafs* acceptance of hadyah is contrary to the Sunnah. I therefore hesitate to accept such gifts."

(*Ishraafun Nafs* means anticipation by the nafs which expected to obtain a gift.) Hadhrat commented:

"The Hadith does not intend this type of ishraaf. The ishraaf mentioned in the Hadith is that which is followed by dejection if the person does not present a gift. If the *muhda ilayh* is not dejected when the person does not make a gift, then there is no harm."

(5) Someone sent a money order as a hadyah to Hadhrat Thaanvi (rahmatullah alayh). The money order was returned to the sender. Along with the money order the sender had requested the reason underlying certain Shar'i rulings. In reply, Hadhrat wrote:

"As long as we are not well known to each other and congeniality (munaasabat) has not been created, I feel embarrassed to accept a gift. Mutual understanding and munaasabat are acquired by frequent meeting or correspondence. Both these acts are within your control, not in mine. I have not recognized who you are merely by you having written your name. I have therefore returned your money order. The proof of the lack of mutual understanding and congeniality is quite apparent from your letter.
You have asked the reason for the masaa-il (rules of the Shariah), but you have no right for this. Without having established sufficient mutual understanding and congeniality, do not again send the gift. As long as I do not accept the money it does not become my property.

45

As far as the Shariah is concerned, you need have no concern since it remains your property which you may bring into your own use."

(6) A man presented a gift of one paisa (a coin of very little value). He gave one anna and requested the change of three paisa. The anna was converted into four paisa in the gathering and three paisa were returned to him while Hadhrat kept the one paisa. Hadhrat commented:

"There can be no question of riya (ostentation or show) in this gift."

(7) Without consulting Hadhrat a man purchased some sweetmeats from the bazaar and presented it to Hadhrat who indicated his displeasure. Hadhrat commented:

"Since you have bought the sweet meats from here you should have unhesitatingly asked me first. You have spent your money, but the sweet meats are of no use to me. I have no children. My wife and myself do not relish sweet meats. Now it may be distributed only to others although the favour remains on me.
What pleasure can there be in accepting such a hadyah? However, taking into consideration your feelings, I say: Half for me and half for you so that you too may understand the effect of eating something without the heart having been pleased."

(8) A stranger presented a prayer-carpet to Hadhrat. Hadhrat said:

"My practice is not to accept gifts on the occasion of the first greeting, especially from a person with whom I do not have close and informal contact."

The stranger said: "I have brought it by the command of Allah. I was commanded to purchase a prayer-mat and present it to you."

Hadhrat said:
"The command of Allah does come to Ambiya.
It does not come to those who are not Nabis."

The stranger:
"It was inspired into my heart."

Hadhrat: "It has been inspired into my heart to refrain from accepting gifts which are presented improperly."

Stranger: "Show me the proper way."

Hadhrat:

"You present me with a gift and you ask me to show you the way! You have no shame. Do you want me also to become shameless and without honour?"

(9) Once Hadhrat said:

"Whenever the need arises for me to refuse a gift, I start to shiver with fear. Is it perhaps not ignoring of a ni'mat (favour of Allah)? For if it is, bounties from Allah Ta'ala will be terminated."

(10) "After much experience did I formulate principles regarding the acceptance of gifts. I know what transpires in this regard, hence my sternness. Even Hadhrat Maulana Muhamad Qaasim (rahmatullah alayh) who was an embodiment of moral excellence held similar views regarding gifts. He would say:

"A gift which is presented by a person who thinks us to be in need, is not acceptable even though in reality we may be in need. However, the one who presents the hadyah has no right to give us hadyah thinking that we are in need. Gifts given in muhabbat (love and affection) should be accepted."

It was also among the practices of Hadhrat Maulana Qaasim Saheb to refuse gifts which were given to him while he was on a journey. Explaining his reason for this, he said:

"On seeing us, the urge to present the gift entered into the heart. It is, therefore quite possible that the gift was not motivated by true muhabbat. It is also possible that muhabbat may be the motive, but the gift was given in a moment of enthusiasm. After the dissipation of the enthusiasm it is possible that the giver may regret (his act of having given a large amount)."

These men are wise men. There is great wisdom and knowledge in their statements "

(11) Frequently people tender gifts (of money) to saintly people while making musaafahah (shaking hands). This is highly improper and wrong. Musaafahah is an act of pure ibaadat.
Worldly considerations should not be mingled with it.

(12) A man was presenting a tasbeeh (rosary) to Hadhrat. Another person who was looking at the beautiful tasbeeh enquired the price of it. Hadhrat said:

"When a hadyah is presented the value should not be asked. This is among the etiquettes of hadyah. The giver is displeased by this on account of possibility that the gift will not be appreciated if it is of little value."

THE AADAAB OF INTERCESSION

(1) The way adopted to intercede (on behalf of another) should not in any way curtail the liberty of the one with whom you are interceding. Nowadays, intercession is in fact compulsion. Indirect pressure is applied. A man will take advantage of his prominence or rank to compel another to submit to his request. This is not intercession. Such intercession is not permissible.

(2) If someone extracts service, etc. from another on the strength of his relationship with a man of prominence or rank and it becomes discernable that the service or aid is not offered freely and wholeheartedly, but has been forthcoming solely on account of the relationship which the taker of the service enjoys with some prominent person, then acceptance of such aid or service is unlawful. As a result of the relationship, the one who supplies the aid entertains the notion that if he does not provide the requested assistance, the man of prominence will be displeased. Thus, to make a request to someone to fulfil a need or supply some aid on this basis is haraam.

(3) In any matter, intercession should not be made without having made investigation.

(4) It will be permissible to intercede on behalf of another if the work or deed happens to be a waajib *(compulsory)* act.

(5) It is not permissible to impose any kind of pressure, direct or indirect, on the person to whom the intercession is directed.

(6) In actual fact, intercession *(sifaarish)* is a branch of *mashwarah* (advice) which cannot be imposed on anyone.

(7) If a person rejects the intercession, he will be acting fully within his rights. It is improper to take offence if one's intercession is not accepted.

(8) If by indications one realizes that the intercession cannot be rejected, e.g. the person is under some obligation, hence he has no alternative other than complying, then such intercession is not permissible.

MALFOOZAAT PERTAINING TO INTERCESSION

(1) A father, bringing along his son, commenced to complain about a certain maktab (elementary Deeni school). He complained that the principal had expelled his child. I (Hadhrat Thaanvi) explained to him nicely that I have no say in that maktab. The man commented: "I heard that you are the head of

that maktab." I informed him that my only relationship with the maktab was that the salaries were given via myself. I have no say in the management of the maktab. The man again started to complain about the principal. I told him that there is no beneficial result in this conversation other than gheebat. After a while, when he was about to leave and shake hands, he repeated his complaint and accused the principal of having been unjust for having expelled his son. In view of the fact, as mentioned earlier, I had informed him of the actual position and had stopped him from continuing the discussion of the complaint, I was very much perplexed by his repeated renewal of the complaint, hence I questioned him with some abruptness. He attempted to present some excuses, but all futile and in vain. He departed in this very condition.

(2) Hadhrat Bareerah (rahiallahu anha) was an emancipated female slave. While she was yet a slave she was in the Nikah of Hadhrat Mugheeth (radhiallahu anhu). On being emancipated she invoked her right of abrogating the Nikah. Hadhrat Mugheeth loved her dearly, hence he wandered around the streets sobbing at the separation. Rasulullah (sallallahu alayhi wasallam), overcome with pity, interceded on his behalf and advised Bareerah:

"O Bareerah! Marry Mugheeth."

The reality and nature of intercession will become apparent from the ensuing discussion. Hadhrat Bareerah asked:

"O Rasulullah! Is this a command or an intercession?"

Indeed, her question was wonderful and subtle. In reply, Rasulullah (sallallahu alayhi wasallam) said:

"It is an intercession."

Bareerah said: "I do not accept it." Rasulullah (sallallahu alayhi wasallam) remained silent. Let some mureed today say to his shaikh that he does not accept his (the shaikh's) intercession. The peer (spiritual guide) will quickly retort that the mureed has become a renegade.

Nowadays spiritual mentors should not intercede. It has become common nowadays to accuse one of refusing to assist even verbally when one refuses to intercede on account of the general corruption prevalent today. One is accused of being miserly. Truly, it is easier to spend wealth but where I detect that a person will accept the request on account of our pressure, then to make an intercession seems like maut (death) because o

50

the suspicion that the person may sustain some loss by having been constrained to act according to the intercession.

(3) A gentleman said to Hadhrat Thaanvi (rahmatullah alayh):

"I wish my son to learn dentistry. If Hadhrat will write a letter of intercession to the dentist in Lahore, it is hoped he will pay greater attention."

Hadhrat replied:
"I have no objection in writing the letter. But the main thing is that there has to be *munaasabat* (congeniality) between the teacher and the pupil. It is not proper to first apply the pressure of *sifaarish* (intercession). The consequence is that whether one approves or not and whether there is *munaasabat* or not. one is constrained to act accordingly. If an intercession is first made, then the conditions which he (the particular dentist) normally stipulates for acquiring this profession cannot be applied freely on account of his liberty having been curtailed by the intercession. Anyway, commence the work. Afterwards I shall intercede for special attention. On the contrary, an intercession in the very beginning will constrict his heart. If all things are done correctly on the basis of principles then there is no difficulty and no perplexity."

(4) Although those who wish me to intercede are not favourably disposed to my way of intercession, nevertheless, I regard transgression of this method (of mine) as a violation of the Shariat. People request that I should write the intercession in forceful terms to apply pressure so that the request is accepted. Since when is it ever permissible to apply pressure on others? How can a person be pressurized into acceptance of the request? My abstention from this pressurizing method is described as *bukhl* (miserliness) by people. In reply I say: To benefit a person is Mustahab. But to impose a difficulty on a person is haraam.

(5) A newcomer arrived and requested Hadhrat to intercede on his behalf in some matter. Hadhrat said:

"Regarding intercession first listen to an introduction. Allah Ta'ala had commanded Nabi Musa (alayhis salaam) to go to Khidr (alayhis salaam) for the purpose of gaining knowledge (in a certain branch of esotericism). When Musa (alayhis salaam) met Khidr (alayhis salaam), he (Khidr) asked the reason for his coming. Musa (alayhis salaam) replied: `May I follow you so that you teach me of the knowledge which has been imparted to you?' Inspite of Khidr's knowledge being insignificant compared to the knowledge of such a

51

great Nabi as Musa (alayhis salaam), the latter said: 'May I follow you.......' It is noteworthy that Musa (alayhis salaam) did not say: 'I have been sent by Allah Ta'ala'. If in fact Musa (alayhis salaam) had mentioned this, it would have amounted to a very high category of intercession. From this should be understood that the type of intercession which one is nowadays required to write out, sometimes weighs heavy on another person. Truly speaking, the Ambiya are the true repositories of true knowledge. It is most significant that Musa (alayhis salaam) did not reveal that Allah Ta'ala had sent him because on hearing that his arrival was by the command of Allah, Khidr (alayhis salaam) would not have had any liberty to speak freely or to stipulate any conditions. Thus, Khidr (alayhis salaam) had freely imposed conditions on Musa (alayhis salaam). We learn also from this episode that one should not 'attempt to derive benefit from someone's companionship without his consent. From this it is learnt that the practice of some visiting students to join in classes without consent is erroneous."

THE AADAAB OF TRAINING CHILDREN

(1) Playfully do not do any act with a child which may be a danger to life or limb, e.g. in playfulness do not fling a child up in the air; do not playfully hold its hands and suspend it from a window, etc.

(2) Do not playfully chase a child, for perhaps he may slip and hurt himself.

(3) Do not speak shameful things in the presence of children.

(4) While the thawaab is considerable for training children in general, caring for and training girls are acts of greater merit and more thawaab.

(5) When training children neither be too strict (harsh) nor too lax.

(6) Children should be taught not to eat things people give them. They should bring such things home and eat them in the presence of their parents if they consent.

(7) Teach them to wash their hands before eating and to eat or drink with their right hands.

(8) Inculcate in them the habit of eating less so that they are saved from sickness and greed.

(9) Inculcate in children the habit of cleaning their teeth, especially with a Miswaak.

(10) Teach them to refrain from asking any of their needs from anyone other than their seniors (parents, grand-parents, etc.).

(11) Teach them never to accept gifts from anyone without the consent of their elders.

(12) Do not assume that they will automatically acquire manners and etiquette when they have grown up. Inculcate good character in them from a tender age. No one learns of his own accord. By reading they will gain the knowledge of good culture, but still they will lack the essential training which was denied to them in childhood. Lack of training will result in the grown-up children always behaving unculturally. Furthermore, they will, without thinking, cause difficulties and inconvenience to others.

(13) Teach children to act with shame, especially when answering the call of nature. They should not reveal themselves to others.

(14) When your child has wronged someone or is at fault, never act partially. Do not side with your child, especially in his presence. To do so is to corrupt his character.

(15) Be watchful of your children's behaviour towards servants and the children of servants. Ensure that they do not trouble the servants or their children. On account of their inferior social rank, they may not complain, but in their hearts they will curse. Even if they do not curse, the misfortune of sin and injustice will be tasted.

(16) As far as possible, endeavour that they learn under suitably qualified teachers.

(17) Do not punish them while in anger. Either, remove them from your presence when you are angry or go away. Later, when the anger has subsided, reflect thrice and then only mete out appropriate punishment.

(18) When the need arises to punish, do not use a heavy stick nor fists. Do not kick the child nor slap it in the face. Also do not hit on the head.

(19) Teach children the full names of their parents and grandparents as well as their addresses. Now and then ask them about this so that they remember. The benefit of this is that, Allah forbid, should they get lost, they will be able to state their identity to the one who finds them. In this way they will be returned home.

(20) Children who are studying should be given such nutrition which is good for the brain.

(21) When the need arises for girls to leave the home precincts, do not adorn them with jewellery.

(22) Emphasise to girls that they should not play with boys. The character of both boys and girls will be corrupted by such intermingling.

(23) If a boy from another house comes to your home, instruct the girls to go out of sight even though the boy may be small.

(24) If any children come to you for education, do not take service from them. Treat them like your own children.

(25) Teach children not to face the Qiblah in the toilet nor to turn their back towards the Qiblah in the toilet. Teach them the rules of *tahaarat* (purification) of cleaning themselves in the toilet.

(26) Do not take children along to invitations. Many people do so. Their habits are corrupted by doing so.

(27) When a child is obstinate in demanding a thing, do not fulfil its demand.

MALFOOZAAT PERTAINING TO CHILDREN

(1) The practice of employing unqualified teachers for the elementary education of children is erroneous. People labour under the impression that the elementary kitaabs are simple, hence there is no need for a highly qualified Aalim. I say that for elementary education there is a need for a highly qualified expert.

(2) Most people make no proper arrangement for the training of children during their childhood. They say: `They are still kids.' Habits are inculcated during early childhood days. Habits inculcated in childhood are enduring. Childhood is the time for developing moral character and for inculcating good moral habits and culture.

(3) A person once made a statement of great wisdom. It deserves to be written in gold. He said that if a child requests something, either fulfil the request the same time or, if you have refused the request, then do not fulfil its stubbornness. Even if it then obstinately demands and cries for it, do not fulfil the request under such circumstances. If you submit to the child's

obstinacy, it will develop this habit. Much wisdom is required when training children.

(4) Nowadays people rear their children in the way cows are reared. They are well-fed and fattened. The ultimate end of the fattened cattle is the slaughter-house. Similarly, people feed their children well, adorn them with garments and jewels and rear them in luxury. The ultimate end of such children is Jahannum (hell). In the process the parents are also punished since by their provision of luxuries and abstention from training, the children grew up ignorant of Salaat, Saum, etc. Some unintelligent parents exceed all limits in that they keep their children entirely unaware of all things of Islam.

(5) I am always advising that during school holidays, children who are attending schools should be left in the suhbat (companionship) of Ahlullaah (Saintly persons - the Shaikhs of Tasawwuf). Even if they do not perform Salaat there, at least their ideas and beliefs will be rectified.

Freedom has now exceeded all limits. Such unbridled freedom was not seen among those who acquired western education in earlier times. Pious persons reared and trained them, hence they did not fall prey to unbridled liberalism. Now, the training is under the instruction of westernized persons. The danger for the future is greater. This is a very delicate age, an age to be extremely careful.

(6) Gentlemen! How sad and lamentable is it! There is time for sports but there is no time for moral training. It is imperative that for your children you appoint a time daily for moral training. Just as you have fixed times in the daily programme for various activities, so too, have a time for your child to go daily to a Musjid or an Aalim where he can sit down and acquire Deeni guidance. If such a spiritual guide is not found in your town, then during the holiday season send him to a place where there is such a Buzrug. During the holiday season the child has nothing to do. The unfortunate child during the holiday season wanders around day and night, not even performing Salaat nor fasting. But the parents remain blissfully happy on account of themselves being regular with Salaat and Saum. However, they remain unaware that on the Day of Qiyaamah they will enter Jahannum along with their children since they were the actual cause of their offspring's deflection from Islam. These are the children of Muslims.....children who have been reared in the laps of Muslim ladies, but will be assigned to Jahannum. You are happy that you have made your child a B.A., a M.A. But, you have left them on the brink of Jahannum. The eyes have become so blind that the Road leading to Jannat is not visible.

THE AADAAB OF CORRESPONDENCE

(1) Do not read the letters of others. If a letter is not intended for you, do not read it.

(2) Do not read any correspondence which is in front of a person. Perhaps the correspondence was meant to have been kept hidden from you. Even if the papers in front of a person happen to be printed matter (not letters), then too, do not read them. It is quite possible that the person concerned does not wish it to be known that he has in his possession that type of literature. (Some people when sitting by an acquaintance or friend have the habit of picking up letters/printed papers, etc which may be in front on the desk. It is not permissible to do so.)

(3) Write very clearly. The topic should not be expressed ambiguously.

(4) In each letter write your address fully. It is not the duty of the addresse to remember one's address which may have been furnished in an earlier letter.

(5) If, in a letter, reference is made to a matter which was mentioned in an earlier letter, then include a copy of the earlier letter. This will save the addressee the inconvenience of searching for the earlier letter. Often one cannot even remember the facts stated in the earlier letter. (This rule will not apply where the practice of systematic filing exists, e.g. as we find nowadays in all offices. However, where private persons are concerned, a copy of the earlier letter should be included. - Translators)

(6) Do not write so many questions in a single letter, which pose an inconvenience to the addressee. After receiving a reply, write the further questions.

(7) If the addressee is one who has many occupations, do not encumber him with requests to convey your Salaams to others; similarly, do not impose this task on any of your seniors.

(8) It is disrespectful to write to a person a request pertaining to something, involvement in which is not appropriate for the addressee.

(9) When a reply is wanted, enclose a reply-paid self-addressed envelope.

(10) Do not write illegibly nor in such faint pencil which makes reading difficult. Do not cram the words nor the lines one on top of the other.

(11) It is not permissible to utilize the stationery of one's employers for one's private letters.

(12) Some people, instead of sending a pre-paid self-addressed envelope, enclose stamps to cover postage. This is incorrect. It is necessary to enclose a self-addressed, postage-paid envelope. This will save the addressee the inconvenience of having to procure an envelope, address it and affix stamps to it.

(13) Do not be wasteful with writing paper. If a letter consists of only a couple of lines, do not use the whole page. Tear the blank portion off.

(14) If the paper is of good quality, then use both sides to write on. Do not waste the one side. Allah Ta'ala says in the Qur'aan Majeed: *"Do not waste. Verily, the wasteful one's are the brothers of the shayaateen."*

(15) Do not use extravagant titles or flattery when writing. Be moderate in addressing.

(16) Do not be too brief in writing. Address elders with appropriate titles of respect.

(17) A single letter should not comprise of different topics.

(18) The letter should be written in the language of the addressee.

(19) When there is a need to discuss more than one subject in a single letter, do not write confusingly. Number the subjects and write in different paragraphs.

(20) Explain the question thoroughly or clearly so that the addressee is not constrained to write seeking clarity.

(21) An important letter or a letter for which a reply is required should be sent by post, not with a person who happens to be passing by.

(22) Think before writing a sentence. Do not write whatever you feel. Consider the feelings of the addressee.

(23) Fold the letter neatly and insert it correctly in the envelope. Do not insert it carelessly in such a way that the adhesive on the envelope sticks to the letter as well. This creates a difficulty for the addressee. Sometimes a portion of the letter is torn while opening it.

(24) Do not unnecessarily write lengthy letters. Replying lengthy letters is onerous on the addressee.

(25) It is nonsensical and futile to write a letter regarding a matter which can be stated verbally, e.g. the person concerned resides in the same town and is easily reachable.

(26) When sending a money order indicate the purpose of the money in the space provided for a message. It is an error to desist from stating the purpose on account of a letter which will explain the purpose of the money. Sometimes the letter goes astray in the post and the addressee is left in the dark.

(27) The letters of females should be endorsed with the signature of a mahram male (husband, father, etc.). This closes the door to mischief.

MALFOOZAAT PERTAINING TO WRITING

(1) In a letter someone posed several questions. In the same letter he informed that he was sending a money order of five rupees. In expectation of the arrival of the money order Hadhrat did not immediately reply the letter. The intention was to reply after receipt of the money order so that the receipt could also be sent together. Several days passed by and it is not known for what reason the money order did not arrive. Finally, after waiting a number of days, Hadhrat wrote to the sender (of the letter):

> "Either you should not have informed in your letter of your intention to send the money order or in the same letter you should not have written queries for which replies were required."

(2) From a certain place an insured envelope containing 50 rupees arrived. Without opening the envelope it was not possible to ascertain the purpose for which the money was sent. It was quite possible that after opening the letter I would have discovered that money was intended for a purpose which I was not able to fulfil. In that event I would have had to return the money. It was also possible that the purpose for the money might have been unclear, necessitating a letter of query from me, and until I had not acquired clarification I would have been constrained to hold the money in trust (amaanat). In the event of having to return it, I would have had to unnecessarily undertake the responsibility of returning it. In the past it did happen that without my asking, people had called me to their place and had sent along travelling expenses, but I was unable to go. If the avenue of expenditure for the money was not defined properly or maybe it was defined correctly, but it required investigation in order to dispense the money in the

58

stated avenue necessitating a letter of query from me to the sender, then while awaiting a reply which may be delayed, I would be obligated to him. One who has many duties to attend to is greatly vexed by such things. For this reason I returned the envelope.

With persons of my disposition it is essential to firstly write requesting or seeking permission, then only should the money be sent. Even with those who do not have the attitude which I have, it is meritorious to first write informing them and seeking their permission. Alternatively, when sending a money order specify the purpose of the money in the space provided for a message so that the addressee knows exactly what to do - to accept it or to return it.

(3) The essence of all these aadaab is that others should not be burdened or inconvenienced by any act or statement. There should be no difficulty or perplexity imposed on others.

This in fact is the essence of noble conduct. By remembering this principle there is no need for elaborate explanation. In regard to this principle it is required that one reflect before making a statement or doing an act. Think if your word or deed is not perhaps hurtful to others. By adopting this habit, commission of errors will be less. After a few days of practice the correct disposition will be inculcated. Then there will be no need for reflection. Speaking or acting correctly will become one's nature. In fact, these things are all natural in man.

(4) THE PROHIBITION OF READING THE LETTERS OF OTHERS

Question:
Is it permissible to read someone's letter without his permission?

Answer:
It is not permissible. However, its prohibition is conditional. Among the reasons for this prohibition is the intention of causing harm to the writer of the letter.
The Hadith states:
"A true Muslim is one from whose tongue and hand Muslims are safe."

Revealing the secrets of others is an act of harm or hurt to the persons concerned. In most cases this is the motive for the desire to surreptitiously read the letters of others.

If the desire is not to harm anyone and the letter is read out of curiosity then it will be known as a laghw act which is also forbidden. Allah Ta'ala says in the Qur'aan Shareef:

59

"They (the Mu'mineen) turn away from laghw (futility)."

If the purpose of reading the letter is not the desire to harm nor is it *laghw*, but is motivated by a genuine good intention, then the prohibition will be waived, e.g. parents censoring the letters of their children; an ustaadh reading the letters of his pupils; a shaikh reading the letters of his mureeds or a sultan reading the letters of his subjects in the interests of the safety and security of the land. Such acts of reading are at times permissible and at times necessary. Rasulullah (sallallahu alayhi wasallam) had ordered that the letter of Haatib Ibn Balta-ah be forcibly taken from his messenger.

(5)   From Pakistan came a letter from a person who desired his *islaah* (reformation).   The writer had left one side of the page blank and commenced on another page. In my reply I asked him for the reason for leaving the one side of the sheet blank. Is this not waste? Allah Ta'ala says: 'Verily, the wasters are the brothers of the shayaateen'. After a few days he wrote back saying: 'Your brief comment has reformed me. When even such an insignificant matter falls within the purview of waste and is sinful, then undoubtedly, all other wasteful expenditures will be major sins. I have now abandoned *israaf* (waste.)
        (This particular malfooz is of Hadhrat Maulana Masihullah Saheb, the Khalifah of Hadhrat Maulana Ashraf Ali Thaanvi (rahmatullah alayh)

(6)   Hadhrat Thaanvi wrote a reply on half a sheet and tore off the other half. He commented:

"This extra piece of paper can be used for the purpose of writing ta'weez. If I had not torn it off, it would have gone wasted."

If the paper was sent by the writer (to be used for replying), Hadhrat would make use of the excess paper only if the sender was a close associate. If not, he would return the excess sheet to the sender.

(7)   Even if I write a letter to any of my students for any of my needs, I enclose a prepaid self-addressed envelope.   Why should I impose any inconvenience and difficulty on them especially when the need is mine? This appears in conflict with intelligence.   Some sincere friends even complain to me about this action of mine, saying that there is no need for sending reply-paid envelopes to them. My answer to them is: Brother! This is best. Allow me to remain free and light.

(8)   If worldly people keep up a correspondence with Ulama, then slowly they will develop a love for the Deen. Fear (of the Deen) will not remain in them. Afterall, they are Muslims and Muslims heed admonition.

(9) Above the address on an envelope was written:
     "In the protection of Shaikh Ma'roof Karkhi."

The belief of these people is that by writing thus, the item will be protected.
Take for example this very letter. The sender is under the impression that
his letter can never be lost. Such beliefs are clear-cut shirk (association in
the worship/power/dispensation of Allah Ta'ala).   Ignorant people have
fabricated this type of stories in the names of the Auliya.

(10) When writing a question the words should be few but conveying the full
meaning. Some people pose a question in such a way that if the addressee
is not already aware of the matter, he will not fully understand the question.
This will necessitate the writing of a letter seeking clarification. The question
should therefore be fully explained, but in few words.   (i.e. the question
should not be unnecessarily expanded nor should the writer assume that the
addressee is aware of the matter.)

(11) The condition of educated people today is such that whatever comes to
mouth, they utter and whatever they wish to say, they write. They do not for
a moment exercise restraint nor reflect on the grief and inconvenience they
are causing others by their actions. There no longer remains any culture. If
someone is able to write, but he lacks culture and manners, then this too is a
form of Allah's Wrath. Such a person will only cause grief to others with his
writing since others suffer as a result of disrespect and ill-manners.

(12) It is nonsensical to write a letter when it is possible to convey the
message verbally. The limits are being totally ignored. People are not in the
habit of pondering and thinking before acting. Whatever they feel like doing,
they do regardless of whether their action is irksome, difficult and onerous to
others. They are not concerned about the peace and comfort of others.

THE AADAAB OF ISTIFTAA' (ASKING A QUESTION TO OBTAIN THE RULING OF THE SHARIAH)

(1)   When the need arises to obtain a Shar'i ruling for one's practical
purposes, not for debating and arguing, then pose the question to a reliable,
authoritative Aalim on whom you have confidence.

(2) Ask only the *mas'alah* (the rule or the law). Do not ask the *daleel* (the
proof of the rule or the basis on which the ruling is given).

(3) Once a question has been posed to a reliable and an authoritative Aalim, do not unnecessarily ask the same question to another Aalim. If, despite having taken into consideration the aforementioned facts, you are not satisfied with the answer, then refer the matter to another Aalim of the same qualifications and attributes. If his answer contradicts the answer of the first Aalim, do not refer it to him (the first Aalim) nor inform the second Aalim of the reply of the first Aalim. Fear Allah Ta'ala and remembering the Reckoning of the Aakhirah, act according to the answer which satisfies you. This act of choosing between the two contradictory rulings for one's practical purposes may be resorted to only if one had heard or learnt of something conflicting against this view prior to having referred it to another Aalim.

These are the aadaab which should be remembered whether the istiftaa' is written or verbal.

(4) The question should be posed very clearly, without ambiguity, and so should be the writing: clear and legible.

(5) Do not include futile and unnecessary statements in the question.

(6) Write your name and address clearly. If several letters are written to the same place seeking answers, then write your name and address on each letter.

(7) Send sufficient stamps to cover postage on a suitable self-addressed envelope.

(8) If several questions are asked, do not write these on a postcard.

(9) Number the questions and keep a copy by you.

Inform the addressee that you have a copy of the letter, hence he should not take the trouble of repeating the questions in his answer.

ERRORS IN GENERAL

(1) Some people refer the same question to several places. Sometimes different answers are received. They are then faced with the dilemma of adopting one of the conflicting answers. Alternatively, they simply adopt the ruling which appeals to their *nafs*. This attitude sometimes develops into a habit and the motive for posing questions is merely to obtain a ruling to soothe the nafs. It is quite obvious that such an attitude is contrary to piety and is purely obedience to the desires of the *nafs*. In addition it constitutes mocking at the Deen.

(2) Sometimes the answer of one Aalim is conveyed to another Aalim. In view of temperaments differing and because of the style of the narrator in conveying the answer, sometimes an inappropriate statement or word slips from the mouth of the one to whom the answer has been conveyed. Then, in turn this statement is conveyed to the first person who had answered the question. In the passage of such messages and statements to and fro, words and meanings are changed by the carriers of the comments. In this manner the flames of a great controversy are ignited.

(3) One error is to ask unnecessary questions.

(4) It is wrong to ask for the *dalaa-il* (proofs or basis) of the *masaa-il*. Academic knowledge is necessary for a correct comprehension of the *dalaa-il*. Since this is lacking, the dalaa-il are not properly understood by laymen. When the Aalim refuses to provide the proofs, the questioner interprets the refusal as ill-manners.

(5) Another error is to acquire a *fatwa* (ruling) merely to substantiate one's views which one had presented in a discussion. The fatwa is then displayed to the antagonist merely to silence him. In turn he writes for a fatwa to substantiate *his* case. In this manner a tug of war, leading to mutual dispute, rivalry and ill-feeling is initiated.

THE AADAAB OF THE MUSJID

(1) Do not perform Salaat in such a place in the Musjid that the free movement of the musallis is impeded, e.g. performing Salaat at the entrance, thus preventing others from passing. Take up a position near to the Qiblah wall in a corner.

(2) Do not unnecessarily stand immediately behind someone's back to perform Salaat. The person in front is perturbed by this action.

(3) When removing your shoes, do not shove aside the shoes of others nor remove their shoes from a place in order to put your shoes there. The place occupied by the shoes of a person is the *haqq* (right) of that person. On emerging from the Musjid if he does not find his shoes there, he will become worried.

(4) Enter the Musjid with the right foot, reciting the Masnoon dua. When leaving, come out with the left foot, reading the appropriate Masnoon dua.

(5) Maintain silence inside the Musjid and sit down respectfully. Before sitting down, perform two raka'ts Tahyatul Musjid Salaat. When visiting the

63

same Musjid several times during the day, performance of Tahyatul Musjid once will suffice.

(6) Do not stare about the Musjid. You are in the Court of Allah Ta'ala, hence sit with fear and in humility, engaging yourself in Salaat or Thikr.

(7) Do not recite anything loudly inside the Musjid. This disturbs and detracts the musallis.

(8) Do not indulge in worldly conversation.

(9) Do not become involved in any worldly activity, e.g. buying, selling, worldly meeting, in the Musjid.

(10) Do not enter the Musjid without wudhu.

(11) Maintain silence even in the wudhu khaanah (ablution block).

(12) Be dressed properly and respectfully when coming to the Musjid. (Some people enter the Musjid with T-shirts, denims or some other disrespectful and unlawful style of dress. This is highly disrespectful and is a violation of the sanctity of the Musjid.)

(13) *The Mu'takif* (one who is in I'tikaaf) should not pass wind inside the Musjid. He should go outside just as he does when having to answer the call of nature.

(14) The Musjid should not be used as a short-cut to get to the other side. This is not permissible.

(15) Items which have a bad odour, e.g. tobacco, fish, etc., should not be brought inside the Musjid. Similarly, after having eaten garlic or onions one should not enter immediately. First cleanse the mouth thoroughly. The same applies to those who smoke.

(16) Acts rendered for worldly purposes are not deeds of *thawaab*. Such activities should not be carried out inside the Musjid. This applies to even writing of such ta'weez which are for worldly purposes.

(17) It is disrespectful to unnecessarily climb on top of the Musjid.

(18) The Imaam of a Musjid, after having given the Athaan, should not go to another Musjid for Jamaa't Salaat. Even if he happens to be the sole musalli present, he should perform his Salaat alone in the Musjid. His salaat in his

Musjid is superior because to populate a Musjid is nobler than performing Salaat with Jamaa't.

(19) Do not utilize haraam wealth or haraam objects in the Musjid.

(20) Sometimes spray perfume inside the Musjid. (NB. It is not permissible to use perfumes containing alcohol nor is it permissible to use the type of aerosols in vogue nowadays).

(21) Do not use the Musjid to make worldly announcements, e.g. for a lost item.

(22) Whenever you have the opportunity, go to the Musjid and engage in Deeni acts such as Thikrullaah, Tilaawaat, Nafl Salaat, etc.

(23) It is not permissible to remove any of the Musjid's items or goods for personal use. All the property of the Musjid is Waqf. Every musalli has an equal right in the use of the Musjid items.

THE AADAAB OF THINGS IN GENERAL USE

(1) Anything which is used by a number of persons should be replaced in its original place after use. Replace it in the same place from where you have taken it so that someone else does not have to search for it when required.

(2) Having used an item, e.g. a chair, do not leave it in the way or in a place where it becomes an obstacle for others.

(3) When giving someone an item, do not throw it at him from a distance. Give it in his hand.

(4) When passing something heavy, hot or a liquid or food to another, do not pass it over someone's head. Perhaps it may slip.

(5) If a needle becomes stuck in cloth while sewing, do not pull it out with the teeth. It may break and hurt you.

(6) Do not leave a needle or any sharp or dangerous item on a chair or bed. Somebody may sit or lay down on it.

(7) Do not pick your teeth with a needle or knife. This is dangerous.

(8) Do not suddenly lift a stone which has been lying in the same spot for a while. Sometimes a scorpion, etc., may be concealed thereunder.

(9) Do not throw peels or any other harmful objects in the pathway or road.

(10) During winter wear suitable garments to give warmth. Many females wear insufficient garments during winter. This causes either colds or fever.

(11) Before lying down to sleep, dust the bedding with a cloth. Sometimes harmful insects settle in the blankets.

(12) After having eaten, do not leave without having removed the food. It is disrespectful to leave the food and move off. First send away the food then get up.

(13) Left-overs which you are not able to eat and crumbs should not be thrown into the dirt-bin. Birds and animals eat such food. Put it in a place where animals and birds may acquire it.

(14) Do not throw away a lighted match. First extinguish it.

(15) Do not leave a burning lamp unattended at home. If no one is present, extinguish it.

(16) When handling dangerous items such as a burning candle, boiling water, hot oil, etc., be very careful. (Some people are in the careless habit of leaving a cup of hot tea/water at the edge of the table. A small child may grab it and spill the boiling contents on him. Women are in the careless and dangerous habit of leaving cooking utensils with their handles protruding from stoves. A passing person may bump against the handle and spill the contents with grave consequences. - *Translators*)

(17) Do not purchase unnecessary crockery or utensils. This is wasteful.

(18) Always keep a stock of essential medicines at home.

(19) Along a journey do not eat foods given by a stranger.

(20) On a journey do not accept responsibility of caring for the goods or anything of strangers nor undertake to deliver any letter or parcel for them.

(21) Take additional money with along a journey.

(22) If you are in debt, then remember to pay immediately you can afford something. Pay whatever you are able to.

(23) Do not give such large loans which will put you into difficulties in the event of non-payment.

(24) Do not use medicine without it having been prescribed by a qualified physician, especially eye-drops.

(25) Safeguard and treat with care an object which you have borrowed. After use, return it immediately. Do not wait for the owner to request the return of the item.

(26) Do not use the articles of others without their permission. To do so is sinful. However, if someone did commit this sin, he should return the item to its original place so that the owner experiences no difficulty in locating it.

(27) Have fixed places for your things. Always replace them in their fixed places after use.

(28) Do not lift very heavy objects. Many people suffer life-long ailments and physical dislocation as a result of having lifted very heavy burdens in their younger days. In this regard women should exercise exceptional care.

(29) Do not throw anything, e.g. a pebble, in playfulness. It may strike someone in the eye or hurt another.

(30) If you have to pass in a gathering with a sharp instrument, keep the point or sharp edge down, covered or concealed to avoid accidental injury to anyone.

(31) Do not in jest point a sharp instrument to anyone. This is dangerous and forbidden.

(32) Do not give an open knife in someone's hand. Place it down so that he may lift it himself.

(33) If a hard-pressed person offers an item for sale, do not take advantage of his situation to acquire the article at a ridiculous price. Either aid him or purchase it for a fair price.

(34) Do not cut off a tree which provides shade and rest for people or animals, especially if the tree is not your property. By doing so, people and animals are put to hardship. This results in *athaab* (divine punishment).

(35) The *thawaab* for giving people insignificant items such as salt or a match to light the fire is as much as the *thawaab* one can obtain by preparing the whole meal for another.

(36) Giving a drink of water to someone in a place where water is available in abundance is the equivalent in *thawaab* of having emancipated a slave. Giving water in a place where water is scarce is equal in thawaab to reviving a dead person.

(37) Do not sleep on a balcony or roof which has no protecting barrier around it.

(38) Do not sit with part of your body in the sun and part in the shade.

(39) Do not sleep on your stomach.

(40) When a morsel of food falls from your hand, pick it up, clean it and eat it. Do not discard it in pride. Food is the *ni'mat* from the Divine Court. Respect it and be grateful.

(41) When eating such food falls which does not require the use of all the fingers, use only three fingers. After having eaten, lick the fingers and clean

the plate with the fingers. Do not leave crumbs and morsels in the plate or scattered on the cloth. In cleaning the fingers in this way, *barkat* increases.

(42) It should be impressed on every member of the household that whenever something, e.g. food, is presented by someone, they should return the utensils immediately.

THE AADAAB OF A PROMISE

(1) Fulfil a promise made. Do not act in conflict with a promise without any valid reason.

(2) Do not make promises in haste.

(3) Do not make promises pertaining to unlawful things. It is not permissible to fulfil such unlawful promises.

(4) Do not make a promise if you have no intention of fulfilling it.

(5) If a child is enticed with something, it will also be a promise which should be honoured. Hadhrat Abdullah Ibn Aamir (radhiallahu anhu) narrates that one day (while he was a child), his mother called him saying that she had something to give to him. Rasulullah (sallallahu alayhi wasallam) who happened to be present asked:

"What do you intend giving him?"

Aamir's mother replied: "I intend to give him some dates."

Rasulullah (sallallahu alayhi wasallam) commented:

"Verily, if you do not give him anything, a lie will be recorded against you."

MALFOOZAAT PERTAINING TO PROMISES

(1) The mudarris (Deeni teacher) of the Maktab in Jalalabad became ill. The principal of the Maktab requested me to send someone for a few days to teach in the place of the mudarris. To avoid any pressure being exercised on anyone, I informed the principal to come here and himself arrange with one of the students to come over for a few days. If anyone voluntarily agrees to go, he has my consent.

The principal convinced one thaakir (a person who passes his time in Thikrullaah) to take the place of the mudarris for a few days. The thaakir agreed, but said that he would first obtain my consent. The principal meanwhile had left. The following day the thaakir came to me and informed me of his reason for having decided not to go. I told him that he should have explained his reason to the principal. This thaakir had made a promise to go on condition I consented. Now by refusing to go, the principal will labour under the impression that although the thaakir wanted to come, I had prevented him from so doing. "Do you want an accusation to be levelled against me? This act is extremely improper. Now go to Jalalabad and explain to the principal that I have given you permission, but you are unable to be present because of a certain reason. It is indeed very bad to cause suspicion against others".

(2) Someone requested some surmah from Hadhrat. He did not promise that he would give it. Instead he said: "Send a child and I shall give it to him." A child was sent after Zuhr and Hadhrat gave the surmah. Hadhrat commented:

"Acting according to principles and methodically, everything proceeds well. People describe this system as strictness. If I had said: I shall bring the surmah, and then forgotten about it, but was later reminded about it, then it would have been violation of a promise as well as a delay in fulfilling the request. But in this method which I had adopted the work was done with ease."

THE AADAAB OF QARDH (LOANS)

(1) Do not borrow from such a person who is unable to refuse inspite of not being disposed to lend. Whether it be Qardh or Aaryah do not borrow from him if by some signs or indications you are able to discern that he is not well-disposed to lend. (Qardh is a loan of cash. Aaryah is an item which is borrowed for a short while.) If it is a person whom you know will not regard it onerous or difficult to give the loan or he may regard it onerous but is one who will not readily refuse, then a loan may be sought from him.

(2) As far as possible avoid taking a loan. If circumstances compel you to obtain a loan, be concerned about repayment. Do not adopt an uncaring attitude regarding repayment.

(3) If the creditor rebukes or speaks harshly to the debtor, the latter (i.e. the debtor) should adopt Sabr and listen on in silence. The creditor has the right to rebuke his debtor for default of payment.

(4) If you owe anyone anything, be it cash borrowed or an article borrowed, make a note of it as a *wasiyyat* (directive) so that one's heirs will know what to do in the event of one's death.

(5) When repaying a debt, make a dua as well for the creditor and express your gratitude.

(6) If the debtor is in difficulty, the creditor should not pressurize him. He should happily consent to an extension. If the creditor is by the means he should waive the debt or part of the debt for a hard-pressed debtor. There is a tremendous amount of *thawaab* for waiving debts. Allah Ta'ala will further lighten the hardships of Qiyaamah for one who waives debts.

(7) There is greater reward for granting a loan than for giving charity. Consider it, therefore, as an act of goodness and good fortune to give a needy person a loan.

(8) If the debtor is unable to pay and he wishes to make arrangements with another person to assume liability for payments, then readily agree to this arrangement. Do not unnecessarily refuse this arrangement if there is reasonable hope for payment to be forthcoming. Such an arrangement is known as *Hawaalah* in Islam. There is much *thawaab* in it.

(9) Poor and needy persons should not keep in trust (as *amaanat*) any articles of others. It is quite possible that in their moments of need the nafs overwhelms them and they make use of the article or sell it.

(10) When obtaining a loan, keep a record of it and when making payment, then too.

(11) Taking a loan is indeed a very lamentable act. If one dies without having liquidated the debt, the *rooh* (soul) remains suspended, entry to Jannat being blocked.

(12) Loans and debts should not be incurred for the acquisition of items of luxury. Exercise patience and be contented with what you possess. Rasulullah (sallallahu alayhi wasallam) said: "To ask is disgraceful." One who does not detest debt is an unscrupulous person. A debtor who deliberately neglects to pay his debt is a very selfish person. He transfers his burden onto another and then adopts a careless attitude.

(13) The act of postponing payment when one is by the means to pay is an act of *zulm* (injustice). Some people have the evil habit of causing the creditor to run to and fro. They attempt to avoid payment by making false

promises and tendering excuses while they are in position to pay. In the discharge of the right of the creditor they are just not bothered.

THE AADAAB OF ILLNESS, IYAADAT AND TA'ZIYAT

(*Iyaadat* means to visit the sick. *Ta'ziyat* is to visit the home of the deceased to console relatives)

(1) If a person suffers from an illness, wound, sore, boil, etc. located in the region of his private parts, do not ask him about the nature of the illness, etc. It is very embarrassing to do so.

(2) Do not express yourself in the presence of the sick or his family in a manner which makes them lose hope in life. Comfort them by telling them that, Insha'Allah, all difficulty will come to an end.

(3) Should you obtain some information regarding injury, illness or death of a person, do not speak about it until you have reliably confirmed it, especially as far as his relatives are concerned. Never inform them without confirmation. If the information was false, unnecessary consternation and grief would have been caused.

(4) If medical treatment has been exhorted, one should adopt it.

(5) Do not use haraam ingredients in medicine.
(Where a pure and halaal medicine is not available, it will be permissible to use a medicine containing haraam ingredients - *Translators*).

(6) Never use talismans (ta'weez) which are in conflict with the Shariah.

(7) Superstition is a kind of *shirk*. Hence abstain from this.

(8) If the indisposed person is suffering from such an ailment which causes inconvenience to people, he should remain aloof from them.

(9) Do not force the indisposed person to eat much.

(10) A person visiting the sick should not linger around much. He should not engage in unnecessary conversation nor should he enquire from the indisposed person the details of his illness. The sick person is inconvenienced by such behaviour.

(11) Do not inform far-off relatives of slight ailments. This creates unnecessary anxiety.

73

(12) Some people never bother to visit the sick. This is not correct. There is great *thawaab* in visiting the sick.

(13) It is improper for a physician to inform the patient that his illness cannot be remedied or that all hope is lost. Some even specify a time limit for the patient's life.

(14) While people do visit sick relatives and friends they do not visit any sick person purely on account of his being a Muslim. Wherever the opportunity arises to visit the sick, do so even if they are not relatives or friends.

(15) People also accompany the Janaazah of only relatives and friends while they abstain from the Janaazah of a Muslim who is a stranger to them. The Janaazah of any Muslim should be accompanied be the *mayyit* an acquaintance or a stranger.

(16) When going for *Ta'ziyat*, console the family of the deceased. Do not do or say anything to augment their sorrow. Nowadays, people instead of comforting the relatives of the *mayyit*, increase their grief and sorrow by joining them in crying and wailing. On arrival, they sit down to cry. This is not *Ta'ziyat*. On the contrary it is *takleef* (giving hardship to others). They utter statements such as: `I am grieved to hear this news.', `Your heart must truly be shattered.', `Indeed his death is a great loss.' etc. This applies more to women. Their statements on such occasions are poisonous. Their statements are harmful to both the body and the Deen.

(17) When going for *Ta'ziyat* do not enquire about the details of the deceased's illness and circumstances of his death.

(18) *Ta'ziyat* consists of two acts: To console the bereaved and *thawaab* for the *mayyit* (deceased). Everything else besides this is nonsensical and baseless.

(19) The practice of visitors coming from far off, the seventh day, tenth day and fortieth day customs are all baseless.

(20) For people living in the same town the period of *Ta'ziyat* according to the Shariah is three days. After the third day they should not go for *Ta'ziyat*. The aim of *Ta'ziyat* is to console, not to revive the grief and sorrow.

(21) *Ta'ziyat* is permissible after three days for those who are the residents of other towns. Since the person arrives from another town or city, the bereaved person will be consoled by his words of sympathy. In fact, if the

outsider merely sits without uttering a word of consolation, the bereaved may feel hurt and consider the attitude of the visitor as a display of insensitivity. Thus, the Shariat has permitted an outsider to go for *Ta'ziyat* even after the third day while the period of three days is fixed for local residents.

(22) Only very close relatives who are able to console the bereaved should go for *Ta'ziyat*. Close friends from whose' companionship the bereaved derives comfort should also go.

(23) When consoling the bereaved, do so with statements such as: *'Whatever has happened, has happened. Crying will be of no avail. Act in the interests and benefit of the mayyit. Recite the Qur'aan Shareef, perform Nafl and make Thikrullah so that the thawaab reaches the mayyit. Make dua of forgiveness on behalf of the mayyit. Have confidence that he is entering Jannat where the comfort is greater. After a time we too shall depart and will meet up with the mayyit'.*

THE AADAAB OF PRESENTING A REQUEST

(1) When going to someone with a need or request, state this immediately on meeting him. Do not wait for you to be asked. Some people going with the intention of asking something, on being asked of the reason or purpose of the visit say that they had come merely to meet. Afterwards they present their need at inopportune times which causes much inconvenience.

(2) When the person to whom you have made your request, be it of a Deeni or worldly nature, questions you, do not answer ambiguously. Do not confuse him.

(3) Do not ask a need from such a person who you know feels obligated to comply even though he may not be disposed to assist.

(4) Some people will present their request for fulfillment at the exact time of their departure. The host finds it difficult to comply at such an inopportune time.

(5) If you have been told to come at a certain time for fulfillment of the need, then be there at the appointed time.

(6) If you have a request to be made to a particular person and coincidentally he makes an appearance, do not ask him at that time. Ask him at another time. He may gain the impression that by visiting you he will be put to the difficulty of fulfilling your requests.

THE AADAAB OF EATING

(1)   While eating do not mention such things which nauseate or are repugnant to others. People of delicate disposition are disgusted with such behaviour.

(2) Do not spit or clean your nose in close proximity of people eating.

(3) When there is the need to bring more food to the guests do not remove the utensil, but bring in another utensil.

(4) Before and after eating, wash the hands.

(5) Recite Bismillaah when commencing to eat.

(6) Eat and drink with your right hand.

(7) Eat in humility. Do not lean against something in the style of proud people when eating.

(8) All should eat together. There is more *barkat* in this way. (However, it is permissible to eat alone as well. - *Translators*)

(9) Eat from in front of you. However, if in the tray or utensil there is a variety of things, then you may eat from any side.

(10) If the food is less and the people present are many, then do not eat to satiation.

(11) When foods such as sweetmeats, grapes, dates, etc., are served, take one at a time. Do not take two at a time. Doing so displays greed and lack of culture.

(12) Where there is no need to use all fingers, eat with three fingers.

(13) After having eaten lick off the food from the fingers.

(14) If a morsel of food drops from the hand, pick it up, clean it and eat it. Do not throw it away on account of pride. Do not think that it is against your dignity to do so. Food is the bounty of Allah Ta'ala. Value it and appreciate it.

(15) If you have completed eating before the others seated with you, continue nibbling here and there to convey the impression that you are still

76

eating. Do not put the others to shame by stopping completely. Those who have not completed may do likewise.

(16) After having eaten, clean the plate out thoroughly. Do not leave crumbs, etc. in the plate. There is *barkat* in cleaning out the plate with one's fingers.

(17) If for some reason you are constrained to leave while the others are still eating, excuse yourself.

(18) When having eaten, do not get up while the food is still spread on the eating-cloth. First wait for the food to be removed, then get up.

(19) After having eaten express your *shukr* (gratitude) to your *Raaziq* (Provider). Recite the appropriate Masnoon Dua.

(20) Similarly, after drinking water recite the Masnoon Dua.

(21) It is haraam to eat from utensils of gold and silver.
Similarly, it is not permissible to use silver or gold cutlery.

(22) Cover foodstuff which is sent to others.

(23) Do not stand and eat nor drink whilst standing if there is no valid need for this.

(24) Do not drink water in a single gulp. Remove the cup from your mouth when taking breath.

(25) Do not drink from the broken or chipped side of a cup.

(26) When passing food or water to a number of people, start from the right side. (This should be the practice even if a small child happens to be sitting on the right side.)

(27) Gather bones and peels to one side. Do not spread these all over the cloth.

(28) Do not leave foodstuff uncovered even for a short while.

AADAAB OF ISTINJAA

(Istinjaa is to purify oneself after answering the call of nature.)

(1) In the toilet use water to purify the affected parts.

(2) Enter the toilet with the left foot and emerge with the right foot.

(3) Before entering the toilet recite the Masnoon Dua.
Similarly, recite the Masnoon Dua after having emerged.

(4) Do not enter the toilet bare-headed.

(5) Abstain from talking while in the toilet.

(6) Do not cough or clear the throat unnecessarily inside the toilet.

(7) Do not recite anything inside the toilet.

(8) Do not take into the toilet any paper or object on which is written an aayat of the Qur'aan, any Hadith, name of Allah or of an Angel, or Nabi or Saint. However, if such an item is wrapped in a cloth and kept in the pocket, then it will be permissible.
Similarly, if a ta'weez is thoroughly wrapped up it will be permissible to have it on one's person in the toilet.

(9) It is *Makrooh* (detestable) to stand while urinating.
However, this will be permissible for a valid reason.

(10) When relieving oneself in the toilet do not be entirely in the nude.

(11) Use the left hand when cleaning yourself in the toilet.
It is *Makrooh* to use the right hand.

(12) Do not use cloth, writing paper, newspaper or any material the purpose of which is not for toilet use nor any impure object for cleansing oneself in the toilet. Istinjaa should be made with soft clay-stone which is absorbent and which has cleansing properties. (It is permissible to use toilet paper. - *Translators*).

(13) Do not face the Qiblah in the toilet nor have the back towards the Qiblah.

(14) When having to answer the call of nature in an open veld, etc., sit as concealed as possible and as far away from the gazes of people as possible. Do not expose yourself to others in the slightest way.

(15) Do not relieve yourself along the road nor in the shade of a tree. People taking rest under trees will be highly inconvenienced and put to difficulty.

(16) Do not urinate in a hole in the ground, for perhaps it is inhabited by some poisonous animals (snake, etc.) which may suddenly emerge.

(17) Do not urinate in stagnant water no matter how abundant it is.

(18) Do not urinate in such a place or in such a way that urine splashes against you. Rasulullah (sallallahu alayhi wasallam) said that carelessness in this regard results in punishment in the grave.

(19) Do not urinate in the bathroom.

(20) When having to relieve yourself outside, do not face the sun and the moon nor against the wind.

(21) When going into the toilet remove your ring on which there is an inscription bearing the Name of Allah or of Rasulullah (sallallahu alayhi wasallam).

AADAAB OF PARENTS

Ahaadith pertaining to parents:

(1) Service to parents result in increase in rizq (earnings, livelihood) and in longer life.

(2) A gaze of love and mercy cast at parents is the equivalent of an accepted Hajj.

(3) Service to parents is superioi to Jihad.

(4) By rendering service to parents, one obtains the thawaab of a Hajj, Umrah and Jihad.

(5) Jannat lies under the feet of your mother.

(6) Gazing with anger at one's parents is disobedience to parents.

(7) Disobedience to parents is among the kabá-ir (major) sins.

(8)   He who is disobedient to parents will be disgraced.   (The curse of disgrace is repeated thrice in the hadith).

(9)   Abusing parents is among the major sins, even the utterance of a harsh word or a word of disrespect.

(10) Allah curses the one who displeases his parents.

(11) The one who troubles his parents will be punished here on earth (in addition to the punishment in the Aakhirah).

(12) The one who disobeys his parents and displeases them, will not enter Jannat.. (He will first have to suffer his punishment before being admitted into Jannat).

(13) The Doors of Jahannum are open for the one who disobeys his parents.

(14) A murderer of parents will be among the worst-punished in the Aakhirah.

(15) The pleasure of the parents is the pleasure of Allah and the displeasure of the parents is the displeasure of Allah.

(16) Service to parents is among the noblest acts by Allah Ta'ala.

(17) Parents are either the Jannat or the Jahannum of their children. Cultivation of their pleasure leads to Jannat while displeasing them paves the way to Jahannum.

(18) A mother's dua for her children is accepted with swiftness.

(19) Jibraeel (alayhis salaam) cursed offspring who displease their parents in their old-age.

(20) The best Door to Jannat is one's father. Either guard it or destroy it.

(21) Whoever desires increase in earnings and long life should be kind and obedient to parents. Kindness to parents secures forgiveness for sins.

(22) The calamity of disobeying parents will be experienced before death as well as after death.

(23) Neither the Fardh nor the Nafl Ibaadat is accepted of a person who is disobedient to his parents.

80

(24) Among the major sins, the worst is to commit shirk with Allah Ta'ala. This is followed by the sin of disobedience to parents.

The Story of Alqamah (radhiallahu anhu)

Alqamah (radhiallahu anhu) was a very pious person. He spent his time in Salaat and Saum. At the approach of death he was unable to proclaim the Kalimah Shahaadat inspite of repeated *talqeen* (instruction) by those present. Alqamah's wife sent a messenger to Rasulullah (sallallahu alayhi wasallam) to inform him of Alqamah's grave condition.

Rasulullah (sallallahu alayhi wasallam) enquired whether the parents of Alqamah wer∍ alive. He was informed that Alqamah's mother was alive. Rasulullah (sallallahu alayhi wasallam) asked the aged mother about Alqamah. She replied:

"Alqamah is a very pious person. He passes his time in Salaat and Saum. He performs Tahajjud, but he always disobeys me for the sake of his wife. I am, therefore, displeased with him."

Rasulullah (sallallahu alayhi wasallam) said:

"It will be best for him if you forgive him."

However, she refused. Rasulullah (sallallahu alayhi wasallam) ordered Bilaal (radhiallahu anhu) to gather firewood and to burn Alqamah in the fire. On hearing this order, Alqamah's mother asked in consternation:

"Will my child be burnt in the fire?'

Rasulullah (sallallahu alayhi wasallam) said:.

"Yes! Compared to the punishment of Allah, our punishment is light. I take oath by Allah that as long as you remain displeased with him, neither his Salaat nor his Sadqah is accepted."

The old lady said:

"I make you and all people present witness that I nave forgiven Alqamah.

Rasulullah (sallallahu alayhi wasallam), addressing the gathering, said:

"Go and see if the Kalimah is on the tongue of Alqamah or not."

After returning from Alqamah the people informed that he was reciting the Kalimah. Thus, he left this world with the Kalimah on his lips.

After burying Alqamah, Rasulullah (sallallahu alayhi wasallam) said:

"The curse of Allah is on the one who causes difficulty to his mother. The curse of the angels and the curse of mankind be on him. Allah Ta'ala neither accepts his Fardh nor his Nafl Ibaadat as long as he does not repent and obeys his mother. He has to gain her pleasure as best as he can. Allah's Pleasure depends on the mother's pleasure and His Wrath is concealed in her wrath," (Ahmad, Tibrani).

Relationship With Parents

(1) Never be disrespectful to parents. Do not say a harsh word to them.

(2) Even if parents are unjust, it is not lawful for children to ill-treat, disobey or displease them.

(3) Obey them in all lawful things. If they instruct you to do anything which is unlawful in the Shariah, then politely and with respect and apology decline. Never refuse rudely nor argue with them.

(4) When parents abuse, scold or even beat their children, they should submit to such treatment with humility. Never should they utter a word of disrespect or complaint, nor should they display on their faces any indication of disgust or anger. Bear their treatment in silence and with patience. Make dua for them.

(5) Assist them in all lawful ways even if they happen to be non-Muslims.

(6) Whenever you see them, greet them.

(7) If you are living with them, take their permission before going anywhere. Inform them of your whereabouts.

(8) If you are engaged in Nafl Salaat and your parents call you, break your Salaat and answer their call even if there is no urgency or importance in their call. If you are performing Fardh Salaat and you detect urgency in their call, then break even the Fardh Salaat to answer their call.

(9) Do not call them on their names. Address them with a title of respect and honour.

(10) After their death, make *Dua-e-Maghfirat* for them. Pray for their forgiveness and within your means, practise virtuous deeds with the intention of the *thawaab* thereof being bestowed on them by Allah Ta'ala.

83

(11) Pay the debts of your parents.

(12) If they had made any lawful *wasiyyat* (bequest), fulfil it if you are by the means to do so.

(13) Be kind, respectful and helpful to the friends of your parents.

(14) When entering the private room of parents, seek their permission before entering.

(15) Always be cheerful in their presence.

(16) Speak kindly and tenderly with them.

(17) When speaking to parents, keep your gaze low. Do not stare them in the face.

(18) Do not raise your voice above the voices of your parents.

(19) Be humble in their presence.

(20) When accompanying parents on a walk, do not walk in front of them nor on their right or left side. Walk slightly behind them.

(21) Even in their absence speak highly and respectfully of them.

(22) Do not give preference to the wife over them (this does not apply to the rights of the wife. Where parents instruct their son to violate or discard the obligatory rights of his wife, it will not be permissible to obey them in this case. -Translators).

(23) Always endeavour to keep them happy.

(24) Do not embark on a journey without their permission.

(25) When they question you, do not inconvenience them by delaying your reply.

(26) It is highly disrespectful to refrain from answering them.

(27) If at any time you were disrespectful to your parents, regret your action and hasten to obtain their pardon.

AADAAB OF ELDERS

(1) When you are in the company of an elder, do not embark on any activity without his consent.

(2) When a senior makes a request, execute it and also inform him when the task has been accomplished.

(3) When having any work or any request for a senior, approach him directly. Do not forward your request via an intermediary.

(4) Do not extract any service from your seniors (be it your Shaikh, Ustadh or other relatives).

(5) When inviting your Shaikh or Ustadh (for meals) and it is your intention to invite his associates as well, then do not invite them via your Shaikh/Ustadh. Do not tell him to bring along so and so. Do the inviting yourself directly to those whom you intend to call. However, take his permission before inviting his associates. The associate who is invited should seek the consent of the Shaikh/Ustadh before accepting such an invitation (i.e. where the Shaikh has been invited too.)

(6) Listen to their talk attentively.

(7) In the Hadith it is said:
"Whoever does not honour our elders is not of us."

Hence, exercise particular care in this regard. Never be disrespectful to seniors. Since juniors no longer respect their seniors, goodness and blessings have become effaeed. Bounties come in the wake of respect.

(8) Disrespect is more harmful than sinning.

(9) True adab (respect) and ta'zeem (honour) are related to love and obedience. A mere external display of etiquette and service is not of much worth.

(10) Do not offer such forms of respect which are irksome and hurtful to others.

(11) Juniors should at all times keep in mind the seniority of elders. Do not regard yourself to be equal to seniors.

85

(12) Juniors should not have the desire that seniors should address them by their titles. They should cherish simplicity and be happy to be called by their names.

(13) In respect and honour offered to elders, keep in mind the respective ranks of the various elders, e.g. a father's right has priority over the rank of the Shaikh (spiritual mentor).

(14) One's Ustaadh and Shaikh hold great rights over one, hence obey them as far as possible. Keep them happy in all ways. They are the guides who guide one out of the darkness and into the light. They set one on the course leading to the True Beloved, viz. Allah Ta'ala. What greater act of kindness can there be than this?

MALFOOZAAT

(1) A village-dweller while speaking to Hadhrat Maulana Ashraf Aii Thaanvi (rahmatullah alayh) was at times making disrespectful remarks. Someone in the *majlis* (gathering) sought to prevent him by making a sign. Hadhrat Thaanvi, observing this, commented:
"What right have you to prevent him? You desire to awe people. You wish to make my gathering like the gathering of Fir'oun. If it is said that he (the village-dweller) was being disrespectful, then understand that Allah Ta'ala has given me a tongue to prevent disrespect. Why do you intrude?"

After this reprimand, Hadhrat said to the village-dweller:

"Whatever you wish to say, do so with liberty."

(2) Hadhrat Thaanvi said:
"Annihilation and submission are best in front of seniors. In their presence abandon your opinion, intelligence, experience and rank. Annihilation means to consider oneself as one of no significance. This is, infact, *adab* (respect).

(3) "Disrespect is the effect of pride and arrogance. The wrath of Allah descends because of pride. Juniors should keep in mind the rank of elders. They should not hold any opinion of their own greatness or rank. Self-esteem is the greatest proof of defective intellect, more so when seniors are present."

(4) "It is not sufficient to merely refrain from thinking highly of yourself. Do not ever regard yourself on par with seniors. The image of a junior who

86

equates himself with a senior will commence declining even though he may be having some rank. His fall will continue. Therefore, it is imperative that he considers himself as being of no significance. He must always bear in mind his insignificance.

(5) "One can only regard oneself to be insignificant if the respect, honour and love of seniors are embedded in the heart. Thus, a person who has such love and respect in his heart will not be neglectful. Neglect and a careless attitude indicate lack of love or respect. If one lacks both love and respect then employ intelligence. Ponder before acting. In this way one will be able to observe the aadaab and huqooq (rights) and abstain from causing hurt and inconvenience to seniors."

(6) "It is lamentable that nowadays the degree of respect shown to spiritual mentors is not offered to parents despite the fact that respect and obedience to parents are Quranic injunctions. If one's father requests one to rub his feet and one's Shaikh (spiritual mentor) orders one to engage in the performance of Nafl Salaat, then according to the Shariah it is *waajib* (obligatory) to obey the father. He who disobeys his father's request and engages in Nafl Salaat in sinful. The relationship of the Shaikh with one is of a lesser degree than that of one's father. It is possible to sever links with the spiritual mentor if for example his instructions conflict with the Shariah. But, it is not possible to sever ties with one's father. His respect is always compulsory on the son."

(7) "In *Islah-e-Inqilaab* I have proved that the rights of parents come first. After parents come the Ustadh then the Shaikh. But people do the opposite. They accord priority to the rights of the peer (spiritual mentor). After the peer they consider the rights of the Ustadh and only then do they consider the rights of parents."

(8) "Some people say that they have no feeling of affection in their hearts for their parents. This indeed is a great weakness and a spiritual disease. The remedy for this malady is to serve them much. By serving them, love for them will be engendered."

(9) "Appreciate, value and remember the Deeni favours which your parents have bestowed to you. Appreciate especially the Deeni education which they have arranged for you. It is necessary to always bring this to mind. Four words of the Deen taught by parents are superior to four whole villages left by them for you."

(10) "If sometimes parents act unjustly, bear their injustice with patience. Reflect on the suffering and hardship which they had to bear since your infancy".

(11) "When the need arises to say something because of some wrong or sinful action of parents, then speak to them tenderly, politely and respectfully. Adopt a soft tone and beautiful terms. Do not adopt a harsh tone and an independent stance nor speak to them by way of raising objections."

(12) "Never hurt their (parents') feelings by any deed or word. This can be ensured by thinking before speaking or acting. Alas! nowadays careless and neglect have become rampant. This is precisely the reason for the abundance of errors which people commit. If one reflects before speaking or acting, errors may then also be committed, but will be very less. Errors committed seldom do not weigh heavily on the heart and mind. By virtue of the habit of pondering, the heart overcomes the slight adverse effect produced by occasional errors. This is the difference between errors in the state of *fikr* (to be concerned) and errors committed as a result of carelessness."

(13) "Do not enter into the private quarters of your parents without their permission." Hadhrat Ataa Bin Yasaar (radhiallahu anhu) narrates that someone asked Rasulullah (sallallahu alayhi wasallam):

"Should I obtain permission from my mother before approaching her?"

Rasulullah (sallallahu alayhi wasallam) replied in the affirmative. The Sahaabi said:

"I live together with my mother in the same house."

Rasulullah (sallallahu alayhi wasallam) said:

'Seek permission'.

The Sahaabi said: 'I have to serve her.'

Rasulullah (sallallahu alayhi wasallam) replied:

`Then too obtain consent. Would you like to see your mother naked?'

The Sahaabi replied: `No'.

Rasulullah (sallallahu alayhi wasallam): "Then obtain permission".

There are various ways of obtaining permission. It will suffice to notify of one's presence in any way.

AADAAB OF THE SHAIKH
(Shaikh here means a spiritual guide.)

(1) Honour and respect Islam and its laws. Be steadfast in the observance of Islam's commands. Pay special care to Islam's teaching of appointing someone as one's senior spiritual (Deeni) guide. Be obedient to him. It is not sufficient to accept him as one's senior merely on paper and addressing him with lauding titles. Obedience and acting in accordance with his (the Shaikh's) *ta'leem* (instruction) are the actual things for practical adoption.

(2) It is necessary for every person to appoint someone (capable and qualified) to act as his Shaikh. This is compulsory.

(3) The necessary condition is to become subservient to the People of Allah (the Auliya) who are the spiritual guides). Cast aside your desires and pride and annihilate yourself in front of them. Act according to their instructions.

(4) In the sphere of *roohaani* (spiritual) training the Shaikh's concern and affection are similar to a father's affection in the sphere of worldly training. In fact, the spiritual mentor has greater affection than even a father. The spiritual mentor executes such tasks which a father is incapable of rendering. He unites man's *rooh* (soul) with Allah Ta'ala. He transforms man into *Aarif* (one who possesses deep knowledge and insight of the spiritual realm) and a *waasil* (one who has attained the goal of Divine Pleasure). Thus in this holy process of spiritual training the bond between the two parties (Shaikh and Mureed) can never be sufficient irrespective of any high degree the association may have attained.

(5) Without being under the guidance of a *Shaikh-e-Kaamil* (a qualified spiritual mentor), there always lurks danger in every step taken. The need is vital to act in conformity with the instruction of a Shaikh-e-Kaamil. Annihilate all your wishes, desires and intentions. Submit yourself to your Shaikh.

(6) Do not raise the slightest objection against the *ta'leem* of your Shaikh. While honouring and respecting all Shaikhs, do not accept for practical adoption their ta'leem. Adopting the *ta'leem* of another Shaikh while ones' shaikh is living is detrimental. Objecting to one's Shaikh's *ta'leem* will deprive one of spiritual progress.

(7) The less one's confidence in one's Shaikh, the less the benefit.

(8) Do not recite poetry in the presence of your Shaikh.

(9) I regard it as disrespectful to write poetry in letters to the Shaikh. There is no harm if such verses are written spontaneously because of momentary enthusiasm and feeling. But poetry should not be written to seniors by deliberate design. It implies the desire to impress and to display one's ability. The student should not adopt such an attitude with his instructor.

(10) One should not sit with a *rosary* (Tasbeeh) in the presence of seniors or in the presence of a person whom one wishes to accept as one's Shaikh. This is contrary to *adab* (respect). It implies a claim of piety.

(11) It is highly disrespectful to display any ability or rank in the presence of one's Shaikh, e.g. to demonstrate one's knowledge. To exhibit one's excellences in order to gain acceptance among the masses is a worse malady. Abstention from this is imperative.

(12) *Noor* (spiritual light) is created by having true respect in the heart for the Auliya. Imaan is strengthened and one's Deen becomes firmly grounded thereby. I greatly fear disrespect shown to the Masha-ikh (plural of Shaikh) and Ulama because the consequences are most dangerous (to Imaan).

(13) When someone speaks ill of those whom you regard as the Masha-ikh, then immediately admonish him. Politely tell him:
"Brother, your attitude grieves me. Do not speak in this way in my presence!"

(For a better understanding of Tasawwuf and the Mureed's relationship with his Shaikh, read the book, Shariat ~nd Tasawwuf by Hadhrat Masihullah. Khan, available from the Publishers. Price: R6 [3.U.S. Dollars].

MALFOOZAAT

(1) Taqwa (piety) has its role in the attainment of *sharh saar*. In this regard, *adab* (respect) too, plays a vital role (i.e. showing respect to the Auliya).
(Sharh Sadr is the heart's state of firm conviction. The mind opens up to fully comprehend the subject. All doubt is eliminated in this state. *Translators).*

(2) Once a man was sitting on the river bank making wudhu. He observed that on his left side on a lower level Imaam Ahmad Bin Hambal (rahmatullah alayh) was seated, also making wudhu. Thinking that it is disrespectful to allow his used water to flow in the direction of the Imaam, he (the man) got up and seated himself at a distance on the left side of the Imaam. After his death Allah Ta'ala pardoned him his sins on account of this act of *adab*. *Adab* is indeed a great asset.

(3) Maulana Gangohi (rahmatullah alayh) said:
"People who criticize, insult and vilify the Ulama of the Deen, their faces in the grave are turned away from the Qiblah."

AADAAB TO BE OBSERVED BY SENIORS FOR JUNIORS

So far most *aadaab* dealt with, concern the respect which people have to uphold for either their contemporaries or their seniors. Some *aadaab* which seniors should observe for juniors will now be mentioned.

(1) Seniors should not be too fussy. They should not lose their temper for every little thing. Just as juniors are disrespectful to you in certain acts, you too, are disrespectful to your elders in some respects. Therefore, be tolerant and once or twice admonish the errant junior tenderly. When soft measures have failed, then sterner measures may be adopted having in view the welfare and betterment of the junior. If you as a senior totally refrain from toleration, you will be depriving yourself always of the benefits of Sabr.

(2) In view of the fact that Allah Ta'ala has appointed you a senior (to guide others), various types of people with different temperaments, dispositions, intelligence and attitudes will refer to you. All cannot be moulded overnight. Remember the following hadith:

"The Mu'min who mingles with people and patiently bears their difficulties (which they cause) is better than one who neither mingles nor bears the difficulties of people."

(3) If you believe that a person will not fulfil your request, then never as' him to do something which is not obligatory in the Shariah.

(4) When someone renders service or makes gifts to you (as the senior) without you having requested for it, then too, take into consideration his comfort and welfare. Do not accept so much service which tires him nor accept gifts of such amount which may be beyond his means. If he invites you for meals, impress on him not to prepare excessive food nor permit him to invite too many of your colleagues.

(5) When expediency dictates that you (as the senior) should display displeasure or sometimes when you are truly displeased, then at some other time gladden the person. If truly you had committed an excess and wronged him, then apologize to him without any hesitation. Do not be proud, for on the Day of Qiyaamah you will be equals.

(6) If in conversation a person's disrespectful attitude distresses you and brings about a change in your temper, then it is best not to talk to him directly. Pursue the discussion via the medium of someone who is capable of understanding and conducting the conversation culturally and politely. By adopting this method, your change of temper will not affect others nor will his disrespect affect you.

(7) Do not exalt nor grant so much proximity to your *khaadim* (voluntary assistant) or your associate that others should hold him in awe. When he (the *khaadim*) conveys to you the stories and affairs of others, forbid him therefrom. If you do not do so, others will become fearful of him and as a result of his narrations you will entertain suspicions on others.

Similarly, when he comes with someone's proposal or he intercedes on behalf of others, then sternly forbid him so that people do not regard him as a medium (to gain audience with you). If they gain the impression that he is your medium, they will be constrained to flatter and please him. They will make gifts to him or he himself will put his requests to them.

In short, you (as the senior) should be in direct contact with people. Do not keep intermediaries. There is no harm in having one or two persons close by as assistants, but they should not interfere at all in the affairs of those who have to deal with you (as the senior).

(7) You (as the senior) should not entrust the arrangements for guests to others. You yourself attend to them, even if you have to undergo much pressure as a result. At least others will have comfort and rest. In fact, it is only natural for seniors to undergo difficulties and sustain pressure.

(8) Some people (seniors) behave arrogantly. They totally disregard others. In so doing they harm people. Even great people are involved in this malady. There is a need to exercise exceptional care to refrain from this type of attitude.

(9) If a senior does not behave affectionately, but adopts arrogance and pride, and resorts to uncalled for dictatorship, then his image and rank will decline.

(10) Service should not be taken from one who is in the employ or under the jurisdiction of another person without first having obtained the consent of the latter. Even if the person in charge happens to be your junior or under your jurisdiction, his consent should still be obtained.

(11) Juniors are to be regarded as the complements of seniors. Both are in need of each other. Sometimes juniors acquire certain excellences from which seniors are totally deprived. Therefore, never despise juniors or those under your authority.

(12) When juniors draw the attention of seniors to the truth, the latter should immediately accept it. The Qur'anic term تَوَاصَوْا means "admonish one another"; "advise one another". Thus, seniors should admonish juniors and vice versa. This Qur'anic form of commanding mutual admonition has alerted seniors to the fact that while they should admonish and advise juniors, they (juniors) too have the right of proclaiming the truth to seniors. Thus, seniors have no justification for taking offence when a junior states the truth to them. On the contrary, they should concede the truth. However, juniors should address seniors with respect and honour when the need arises for them to proclaim the truth to their seniors. Only an intelligent person will adopt the correct attitude.

(13) Acting in an unprincipled manner with even juniors is improper. While juniors should not hurt and inconvenience seniors by word or deeds, seniors too should reciprocate. Nowadays no care is taken to avoid inconveniencing others. The concern is primarily to obtain fulfillment of one's personal motives and needs irrespective of any hurt or harm caused to others in the process.

(14) The *Shaikh-e-Kaamil* (the qualified spiritual mentor) is a person who comforts the *Taalib* (the searcher of Allah) and supports him during his conditions of despondency and frustration. He provides encouragement and solace to the *Taalib*.

(15) People wholly ignore the rights of their wives and children. They are proficient in only exercising dictatorial authority. They do not stop to think

(15) People wholly ignore the rights of their wives and children. They are proficient in only exercising dictatorial authority. They do not stop to think that those over whom they are exercising authority have rights to be fulfilled. They have excluded *Muasharat* (social relationship) from the scope of the Deen. Considerable deficiency exists in this regard. The cause for this lamentable situation is the unconcerned attitude of seniors. They have become unconcerned about the Deen.

(16) So-called religious persons who are deficient in discharging the rights of their associates are in fact unaware of the Deen. In reality they are not religious, even though people regard them as being pious.

MALFOOZ

While I do not issue a *Fatwa* (Deeni verdict), I do advise that the husband should either hold the reins of the home affairs (expenses, etc.) himself or permit his wife to have this control. He should not assign this control to others, whether they happen to be brothers, sisters or even his parents. Handing over control of the home-affairs to others distresses the wife considerably. The husband should handle the home-budget himself or assign it to his wife. Among all relatives she is the one most entitled in this respect.

The rights of the wife are not confined to food and clothing. In addition, it is essential to keep her happy. Her happiness is of such importance that the fuqaha (jurists of Islam) have ruled that it is permissible to speak, even a lie to keep her happy. (By a 'lie' is meant a statement calculated to make her happy even though it be contrary to fact, but as long as the statement does not infringe on anyone's right nor does it bring about any violation of the Shariah, e.g. it will be permissible to express love to the wife even though the husband's heart is devoid of love for her. - *Translators*).

This ruling of the Fuqaha is very significant. The importance of the right of the wife can be adequately gauged therefrom. For the sake of her happiness even Allah Ta'ala has waived one of his rights, viz. his prohibition on lies.

CONCLUSION

I now conclude this discussion of etiquettes and rules on a dictum which is beyond the scope of rules and principles, viz; some of the *aadaab* have a general application. They concern all people at all times. However, associates who are very close to each other-between whom there is no relationship of formality - are excluded from observing certain *aadaab* and rules. Since the realization of the degree of formality and closeness necessary for the relaxation of rules is dependent on intuition and temperament, the fixation of such *aadaab* (for relaxation) will be left to the individual's intuition and temperament.

I now end this treatise with the following verses:

طرق العشق كلها آداب
ادّبوا النفس ايها الاصحاب

(Translation: All ways of love are aadaab (etiquette and respect).
O Friend! impart the lessons of aadaab to yourself.)

AQAAIDUL
ISLAM

Translated by
Maulavi Zahier Ahmed Ragie

The Deen (Islam) can basically be divided into three compiled sciences; *Ilmul-Kalaam* (dialectical theology: developed from *Iman*), *Ilmul-Fiqh* (jurisprudence: developed from Islam) and *Ilmul-Tasawwuf* (Islamic mysticism: developed form *Ihsan*).

This book is based upon *Ilmul-Kalaam,* a clear and categorical tenets of the Holy *Qur'an* and *Ahadeeth.* The beauty of Islam lies in the fact that has a clear set of beliefs, which projects a system easy and practical for a successful life here and in the life hereafter.